CRIMINAL JUSTICE IN CALIFORNIA

ELLEN G. COHN
Florida International University

PEARSON
Prentice Hall

Upper Saddle River, New Jersey 07458

Publisher: Stephen Helba
Executive Editor: Frank Mortimer, Jr.
Assistant Editor: Sara Holle
Production Editor: Barbara Cappuccio
Director of Manufacturing and Production: Bruce Johnson
Managing Editor: Mary Carnis
Manufacturing Buyer: Cathleen Petersen
Creative Director: Cheryl Asherman
Cover Design Coordinator: Miguel Ortiz
Cover Design: Denise Brown
Cover Image: Day Williams/Photo Researchers, Inc.

Pearson Education LTD.
Pearson Education Singapore, Pte. Ltd
Pearson Education, Canada, Ltd
Pearson Education–Japan
Pearson Education Australia PTY, Limited
Pearson Education North Asia Ltd
Pearson Educaçion de Mexico, S.A. de C.V.
Pearson Education Malaysia, Pte. Ltd

PEARSON
Prentice Hall

10 9 8 7 6 5 4 3 2
ISBN 0-13-114027-

CONTENTS

	Preface	v
Chapter 1	**The State of California**	1
	Introduction	1
	The History of California	1
	California Today	5
	Notes	6
Chapter 2	**Introduction to California Criminal Law**	7
	The Structure of the Government	7
	The California Penal Code	10
	The Definition and Classification of Crime	11
	Defenses To a Criminal Charge	12
	Sources of Information for Legal Research	15
	Notes	17
Chapter 3	**Index Crimes**	19
	Introduction	19
	Criminal Homicide	19
	Forcible Rape	24
	Robbery	26
	Assault and Battery	28
	Burglary	31
	Larceny-Theft	32
	Motor Vehicle Theft	34
	Arson	35
	Hate Crimes	38
	Notes	39
Chapter 4	**The Police in California**	41
	Introduction	41
	Local Policing	41
	County Policing	44
	State Policing	47
	Police Training	50
	Notes	52
Chapter 5	**The Court System in California**	53
	United States District Courts	53
	The California Supreme Court	53
	California District Courts of Appeal	55
	Trial Courts in California	56

	Court Administration	57
	California Criminal Court Procedures	60
	Notes	68
Chapter 6	**Sentencing in California**	71
	Introduction	71
	Types of Sentences	71
	When Sentencing Occurs	72
	Determinate and Indeterminate Sentencing	72
	Aggravating and Mitigating Circumstances	74
	Concurrent Versus Consecutive Sentences	76
	Intermediate Sentences	77
	Victim Rights and Services	78
	Notes	82
Chapter 7	**Capital Punishment in California**	83
	The History of Capital Punishment in California	83
	Capital Punishment in California Today	85
	The Cost of Executions in California Today	89
	The Execution Procedure in California	90
	Notes	92
Chapter 8	**Corrections in California**	95
	Introduction	95
	Jails in California	95
	Prisons in California	97
	Parole in California	102
	Probation in California	105
	Victims' Rights	106
	Becoming a Correctional Officer	106
	Notes	107
Chapter 9	**The Juvenile Justice System in California**	109
	Introduction	109
	The Juvenile Justice Process in California	109
	Juvenile Supervision in California	114
	Notes	116
Chapter 10	**Drugs and Crime in California**	117
	Introduction	117
	The Availability of Drugs in California	117
	California Drug Treatment Courts	118
	The Substance Abuse and Crime Prevention Act of 2000	120
	Notes	120
Appendix	**Web Sites of Interest**	123

PREFACE

This supplementary text will provide you with specific information on the California criminal law and the California criminal justice system. Throughout the text, you will find quotations which have been taken verbatim from various legal documents, including the California Penal Code and the California State Constitution. Any misspellings or other irregularities are reproduced exactly as they appear in the original documents.

I hope that you enjoy this supplement and find it both interesting and informative. If you have any questions, comments, or suggestions, please feel free to contact me via email.

Ellen G. Cohn, Ph.D.
cohne@fiu.edu

CHAPTER 1

THE STATE OF CALIFORNIA

INTRODUCTION

California is located in the western portion of the United States, bordering the Pacific Ocean. The state borders Oregon on the north, Nevada and Arizona on the east, and Mexico to the south. Sacramento is the capital of California. The state bird is the California quail, the state animal is the California grizzly bear, the state flower is the California poppy, and the state tree is the California redwood. The official nickname of California is the "Golden State," which refers to the gold rush of the late 1840s. The state motto is "Eureka", which means "I have found it!" in Greek and also refers to the California gold rush.

THE HISTORY OF CALIFORNIA

Spanish Rule of Florida

California was originally occupied by over 100 different Native American tribes, including the Hupa, Pomo, Miwok, Chumash, Mojave, and Serrano. The tribes, which numbered up to 300,000, were small, spoke different languages, and lived independently. For example, the Hupa Indians lived in the northwestern part of California, the Maidu in the central area, and the Quechan in the southern section of California. This diversity severely limited their eventual ability to mount a combined, organized defense against European discovery and colonization.

The first Europeans to reach California were Spanish explorers. Juan Rodriguez Cabrillo discovered San Diego Bay in 1542. He then continued to explore north, possibly as far as the area that is now Oregon. In 1579, the English explorer Francis Drake sailed along the California coast and claimed the land for England, naming it New Albion. Fearful that they would lose California to the English, the Spanish then sent out exploring parties along the coast. However, actual European colonization of California did not occur until 1769, when the Spanish Franciscans began to establish missions and other settlements in Baja California. Presidios, or military posts, were established at San Diego and Monterey in the late 18th century.

By the early 19th century, Russia also began to show interest in the California region. Russians were involved in fur-trading in Alaska and wanted to move their settlements further south down the Pacific coast. The Russians established a fort (Fort Ross) on the northern California coast in 1812. Russian activity in the California region eventually contributed to the 1823 Monroe Doctrine, in which the United States declared that North and South America were closed to European colonization. Russia agreed to limit settlements to Alaska in 1824, although they did not actually leave the California region until the early 1840s.

Between 1769 and 1823, a total of 21 Franciscan missions were founded along the California coast between San Diego and San Francisco, each approximately one day's walk apart. These missions became home to thousands of American Indians. The friars at the missions converted the Indians to Christianity and taught them skills such as farming and weaving. However, they also forced the Indians living at the missions to work long hours and exposed them to new diseases, resulting in the death of almost two-thirds of the native population of the area[1]. By the mid-1840s, most of the mission property had been sold to private landowners and the missions were closed.

Spain maintained a distant rule over California until the onset of the Mexican Revolution (1810-1820). In 1821, Mexico became independent from Spain and in 1825 California (then known as Alta California) formally became a province. Although the province set up its own legislature, Mexico sent a series of governors to California. Rule by outsiders was resented by Californians and there were rebellions against the governors and the government troops. As a result, Mexican rule of California became distant and the area was frequently neglected by the Mexican government.

America Acquires California

America's increasing interest in the region was shown by the arrival of a variety of expeditions into California. The first American land expedition to reach California was led by Jedediah Strong Smith in 1826. Other explorers and trappers soon followed and quickly decimated the population of sea otter and beaver nearly to extinction. The first organized group of American settlers arrived overland in California in 1841 via wagon train. Other groups of settlers soon followed and these new residents expressed their desire to make California a part of the United States. The United States government offered to purchase the land from Mexico, but Presidents Andrew Jackson, John Tyler, and James Polk were all unable to persuade Mexico to sell the area to the United States.

In the mid-1840s, American military forces occupied the area of California. In 1846, the Mexican War broke out. One month later (on June 14, 1846), unaware that war had been declared, a group of American settlers took over the fort at Sonoma, which was being used by Mexico as a headquarters in the northern area of California. This action was called the Bear Flag Revolt, because after capturing the fort, the settlers raised a homemade flag bearing a star, a grizzly bear, and the words "California Republic." After two years of fighting, the United States won the Mexican War and the Treaty of Guadalupe Hidalgo formally ceded California to the United States. California officially became a U.S. Territory on February 2, 1848.

Only a few days prior to the signing of the treaty, gold was discovered at Sutter's Mill, a sawmill located on the American River. News of the discovery spread throughout the country, resulting in a "gold rush" that brought thousands of gold-hunters, or "Forty-Niners," to the region and creating a virtual population explosion in California, particularly in the area near Sierra Nevada. Between 1848 and 1850, the population of California increased from approximately 15,000 to over 100,000. By 1860 it had risen to almost 400,000. Although most prospectors returned to their former homes and occupations after several years in the gold fields, some remained in California and settled permanently in the area, becoming ranchers, farmers, or merchants.

Crime Problems in 19th Century California

The instability and disorder that resulted from the sudden and massive immigration into the region led to serious crime problems in California and resulted in an increase in vigilante justice. Miners who had found gold were frequently attacked and robbed when they returned to the nearest city or town. Bandits followed shipments of gold and attacked wagons and stagecoaches. Claim jumpers illegally claimed mines that belonged to another miner. Others "salted" worthless mines with small amounts of gold and then sold the mines for large sums. Law enforcement was difficult because of the distance between cities. Sheriffs were frequently responsible for enormous territories and often had no jails in which to keep prisoners. One answer to the problem of law enforcement was vigilantes, citizens who grouped together to capture and punish criminals. Many of the vigilante groups were composed of law-abiding citizens who worked to preserve law and order. However, some vigilantism was, in reality, mob action, and involved excessive violence and the deaths of innocent people.

One of the most well-known examples of vigilantism in California is the San Francisco Vigilance Committee, which was formed in 1856 in response to the murder of a United States Marshal named Richardson, and later, of a newspaper editor who was speaking out against the failure of the courts to convict Richardson's murder. The Vigilance Committee had over 6000 members and focused not only on criminal offenders but also on ousting the local Democratic political machine. The Committee eventually entered the political arena and controlled the government of San Francisco for the next ten years.

California as a State

In an attempt to prevent more violence and confusion throughout the state, the military governor called for a constitutional convention. In October 1849, the convention adopted a constitution as if California was already a state, rather than a territory, and in November of the same year the constitution was ratified by the voters. After a lengthy debate in Congress, California was recognized as the 31st state of the Union, on September 9, 1850. As part of the Compromise of 1850, California entered the United States as a free state, without slavery. The first state governor was a Democrat, Peter H. Burnett. The first state capital was located at San Jose; it was later moved to Monterey, Vallejo, Benicia, and eventually settled in Sacramento.

After the Gold Rush, many groups of Native Americans were forced to move to reservations which were often located in infertile and inhospitable areas. In 1872, the Modoc Indians of northern California and southern Oregon, left the reservation they had been given in 1864 and returned to their old lands. Army troops attempted to force the Indians back onto the reservation lands and the Modoc fled to Tule Lake in California. Fighting continued into the following year, while a small group of Modoc held out for five months, until forced to surrender by the Army. Chief Kintpuash of the Modoc, known as Captain Jack, was hanged and the remainder of the tribe was sent to a reservation in Ohio. This conflict is now known as the Modoc War.

In 1852, the California State Prison at San Quentin was opened in Marin County, near San Francisco. It is California's oldest prison. In 1854, a military fort was erected on Alcatraz Island, located in San Francisco Bay. In 1861 a military prison was added to the fort and in 1934, Alcatraz was converted to a federal prison and used to hold some of the most dangerous criminals in the country. The prison was closed in 1963, when the federal government decided that it was too expensive to maintain.

After the end of the Civil War, more and more settlers began heading out to California in search of high wages and the opportunity to purchase land. The first transcontinental railroad system was completed in 1869, linking Sacramento with the Eastern seaboard. Many Chinese immigrants worked as laborers on the railroad and remained in the area. By 1870, the population of California had increased to approximately 560,000. However, between 1870 and 1880, a depression led to a number of bank failures and to widespread unemployment, which many blamed on the Chinese laborers, who were willing to work for lower wages than Americans in California. In 1871, a series of anti-Chinese riots occurred in Los Angeles; more took place in San Francisco in 1877. In 1879, a new state constitution was adopted that included a number of anti-Chinese articles. A year later, the United States Congress passed a law that regulated Chinese immigration to the U.S.; in 1882 Chinese immigration was banned for ten years.

California During the 20th Century

In the early 20th century, California's population continued to increase, particularly in the southern region of the state, as the use of irrigation on desert areas expanded the state's arable farming land. The discovery of both oil and natural gas led to the development of new industries, and mining of gold and other minerals increased the importance of that industry to the state. The motion picture industry was headquartered in Hollywood by 1910.

The Panama Canal was completed in 1914, linking California and the eastern United States by sea. The Panama-Pacific International Exposition was held in San Francisco in 1915 and the Panama-California Exposition was held in San Diego in 1915 and 1916. Both events were sponsored by the state as a way of demonstrating the Canal's importance to the state of California. The completion of the Hoover Dam at Boulder Canyon (on the border between Nevada and Arizona) in 1920, was also important to California. The dam was designed to control floods from the Colorado River, and to provide water for both power and irrigation in southern California, as well as in the neighboring states.

In the 1930s, during the Great Depression, several thousand homeless farmers and farm workers headed to California to escape the droughts in Arkansas and Oklahoma. The sudden stream of unemployed people into the state led to the passage of state legislation closing the borders of California to poor people. However, the U.S. Supreme Court later declared this law to be unconstitutional.

During World War II, over 100,000 Japanese-Americans living in California were moved out of the state and into detention camps located in the interior of the U.S. The majority of these people were American citizens. A large number of defense plants were built in California to produce ships, airplanes, and weapons. Many of the people who moved to the state during the war, either as defense workers or members of the armed forces, remained in California after the war, generating another massive population increase and leading to serious environmental concerns, including the problem of smog in Los Angeles and other cities. Water resources also became a significant problem in the

1960s; the state eventually built a system of dams, reservoirs, canals, and power plants to store and distribute the excess water from northern California to the drier areas in the southern part of the state.

The 1960s were also a time of social unrest for the state. The racially-motivated Watts riot in Los Angeles in 1965 caused the deaths of 34 people and resulted in millions of dollars of property damage. The first major anti-war college demonstration in the United States, which was organized by the Free Speech Movement, occurred at the University of California, Berkeley in 1964. The movement to unionize California's mostly-Hispanic farm workers, led by César Chávez, eventually led to the passage of the Agriculture Labor Relations Act, giving all farm workers the right to collective bargaining.

Unemployment rose in California in the early 1970s as a result of cuts in federal military spending in the state. The passage of Proposition 13 in 1978, calling for a $7 billion reduction in state property taxes, resulted in additional revenue losses for the state. The economy took an upswing in the early 1980s, with the help of new federal military aerospace contracts. Santa Clara County became known as "Silicon Valley" because of its importance in the production of high-tech electronics. In the early 1990s, another decrease in federal military spending led to a recession in the state. Recently, however, the economy has improved due to the growth of service industries and other economic activities.

The population of California has increased significantly since the 1970s, at least in part because of the increasing immigration into the state from the Carribean, Latin America, Mexico, Europe, and various countries in Asia. Illegal immigration from Mexico has created additional concerns for the state. In 1986, voters approved a referendum to make English the official language of the state. In 1994, California voters approved the passage of Proposition 187,which banned illegal immigrants from receiving many social services, including public education and free non-emergency medical care. These immigrants were already ineligible for a number of major federal health and welfare programs. A number of lawsuits were filed to block the implementation of Proposition 187 and the courts ruled that many of the provisions in the Proposition were unconstitutional, based on the ruling that immigration regulation is a power reserved for the federal government, rather than one granted to the states. However, one result of the passage of Proposition 187 was to increase the racial tensions already existing in the state. Higher education in California also has not been immune from racial concerns. Affirmative action policies created in the 1970s led many university administrations to create admissions policies that included racial preferences, as a way of increasing minority representation in the state university system. In 1978, the U.S. Supreme Court stated that racial quotas may not be developed, but that race may be considered as one of a number of admission factors. However, in 1996, voters passed Proposition 209 (the California Civil Rights Initiative), which eliminated all racial, gender, or ethnic preference for admission to any state school, as well as for state employment or the administration of state contracts.

CALIFORNIA TODAY

In land area, California is the 3rd largest state in the country, after Alaska and Texas, with a total land area of 155,959 square miles, as well as 2,674 square miles of inland water and 22 square miles of coastal waters over which the state has jurisdiction. Both the lowest and the highest points in the contiguous 48 states are found in California. Death Valley, located in the southern portion of the state is 282 feet below sea level while Mt. Whitney is 14,491 feet above sea level.

California is the most populous state in the country. The 2000 census[2] reported a population of 33,871,648, an increase of 13.8 percent over the 1990 figure and 30 percent over the 1980 census. In 2000, the average population density was 217 persons per square mile. The most populous city in California is Los Angeles, with almost 3.7 million residents in 2000. Almost half the entire population of the state (approximately 16.4 million people) live in the Los-Angeles-Riverside-Orange County metropolitan area. The city of Los Angeles alone had almost 3.7 million residents in 2000. Other cities with a population over 100,000 include Long Beach, Anaheim, Riverside, San Bernardino, Torrance, Pomona, Pasadena, San Diego, Berkeley, and Ventura.

According to the 2000 census[3], approximately 60 percent of the state's population are white, 11 percent are Asian, and 7 percent are black. Over 32 percent of the population are reported as being of Hispanic or Latino origin, although they may be of any race. Most of the population lives in urban areas. Over 26 percent of California residents are foreign-born, more than twice the national figure. Approximately 40 percent reported that a language other than English is spoken in the home. More immigrants settle in California than in any other state in the country, with most coming from China, Japan, and other Asian-Pacific countries.

California has a total of 58 counties. The state elects two United States Senators and 52 members of the House of Representatives, for a total of 54 electoral votes. The current state constitution was adopted in 1879.

NOTES

1. Rawls, J.J. (1984). *Indians of California: The changing image.* Norman, OK: University of Oklahoma Press.
2. United States Census Bureau (http://www.census.gov)
3. *Ibid.*

CHAPTER 2

INTRODUCTION TO CALIFORNIA CRIMINAL LAW

THE STRUCTURE OF THE GOVERNMENT

California law is found in the state constitution and in the California Penal Code. Both have been frequently modified, amended, and altered over the past 150 years.

The first **California State Constitution**[1] was ratified in 1849, almost a full year before statehood was achieved. The current (second) constitution was adopted in 1879 and has been amended over 350 times since then. The California Constitution is the primary law of the state, although it is of course subordinate to the United States Constitution. No criminal law or constitutional amendment enacted in California may conflict with or violate any individual rights which are guaranteed by the U.S. Constitution, the Bill of Rights, any other Constitutional Amendments, or any federal laws. If any part of the California Constitution or legal code is found to be in conflict with the U.S. Constitution or any federal statutes, the California enactment is unconstitutional and must be changed. Conflicts between federal and state laws do occur periodically. For example, in 1996, California voters passed Proposition 215, the Compassionate Use Act of 1996, which legalized the medical use of marijuana by individuals with serious illnesses such as glaucoma and AIDS, when it is recommended in writing by a licensed physician. However, this law is in direct conflict with federal anti-drug laws that regulate possession and use of marijuana.

There are several ways in which the constitution may be amended or revised. These are described in Articles 2 and 18 of the California State Constitution. First, a new amendment or revision of the Constitution may be proposed by the **California State Legislature**, following a two-thirds majority vote in each house.[2] Second, the constitution may be amended through the **initiative** process, which involves citizens of the state presenting a petition signed by a specified number of voters (at least eight percent of the votes for all candidates for Governor at the last election).[3] Finally, a **constitutional convention** may be called for the purpose of revising the entire state constitution. This process requires a two-thirds majority vote in each house of the State Legislature followed by a majority vote in a general election.[4] Regardless of the method used to propose an amendment to, or revision of, the Constitution, each proposed amendment or constitutional revision must be presented separately and no initiative may cover more than one subject. The proposed amendment must then be approved by a majority of the voters in a state-wide election before it becomes law.

Like most states, California has three branches of government: executive, legislative, and judicial. This is specified in Article 3, Section 3 of the California State Constitution.

The Executive Branch

Article 5 of the California State Constitution discusses the state's **executive branch**. The supreme executive power of the state lies with the Governor, who is elected to a four-year term and is limited to a total of two terms. Other members of the executive branch include the lieutenant governor, attorney general, secretary of state, controller, and the superintendent of public instruction. In addition, voters elect a five-member State Board of Equalization to administer important tax laws. All executive officers are elected to a four-year term and are eligible for reelection only once. The governor must, at the time of election, be an elector who is a U.S. citizen and a citizen of the state of California. In California, an elector must be at least 18 years of age; therefore, no one under the age of 18 may be elected to the office of governor. The California Constitution also includes a five-year residency requirement for the governor but, because this requirement conflicts with United States Supreme Court decisions, it is invalid. Requirements for the office of lieutenant governor are the same as for governor.

The governor has the power to veto legislation that has been proposed by the state legislature. However, a two-thirds vote in both houses of the legislature may override the governor's veto. The governor also has the power to make appointments if vacancies occur in many of the offices of the executive branch or the judiciary, and to fill newly created judgeships.

The current governor of California is Democrat Gray Davis, who was elected the 37th governor of the state in November 1998 and re-elected in November 2002. His present term expires in 2006 and he cannot be re-elected.

The Legislative Branch

The **California Legislature** is discussed in Article 4 of the California State Constitution. The legislature is made up of two houses: a 40-member Senate and an 80-member Assembly. Each member of the legislature represents one Senatorial or Assembly district. Senators are elected to a four-year term and are eligible to serve only two terms. Members of the Assembly serve two-year terms and may be re-elected twice. A regular session of the legislature runs approximately two years, beginning on the first Monday in December of each even-numbered year and ending on November 30th of the next even-numbered year. For example, the legislative session that began on December 2, 2002 will end at midnight on November 30, 2004. In addition to regular sessions, the governor may call a special or extraordinary session of the legislature, at which only those subjects specifically presented by the governor may be addressed.

The Judicial Branch

The **Judicial Branch** of the government is discussed in Article 6 of the California State Constitution and contains the various California courts. The highest court in the state is the **California Supreme Court**, which is made up of seven justices, including one chief justice and six associate justices. Supreme court justices are elected by voters at a statewide election and serve twelve-year terms. Only the U.S. Supreme Court may reverse a decision of the California Supreme Court. In addition, the state is divided into judicial districts, each of which has a **district court of appeal**. Justices of these courts are elected by the voters within the given district and serve terms of twelve years. Courts of appeal have appellate jurisdiction over all cases in which a superior court has exercised original jurisdiction, except in those cases where a sentence of death was handed down.

Prior to 1998, California had two levels of trial courts. The lower level trial courts were known as **municipal courts** and had jurisdiction over all criminal misdemeanors and infractions and over some small claims cases and civil lawsuits. Felony arraignments and preliminary hearings were also held in the municipal court in some cases. **Superior courts** were the county trial court of general jurisdiction and had jurisdiction over all felony cases and over those civil lawsuits not under the jurisdiction of the municipal court.

In June, 1998, California voters passed Proposition 220, a constitutional amendment which gave each county the option of merging its superior and municipal courts into a **unified superior court** within the county. This may only be done with the approval of a majority of both the superior and municipal court judges in a county. The purpose of Proposition 220 is to increase the efficiency of the court system, to reduce the frequent duplication of services, and to save money. As of February 2001, all 58 counties in California had voted to unify trial courts. Municipal courts have been eliminated and the superior courts have been given original trial jurisdiction over all cases not specifically assigned by statute to some other court. This includes felonies, misdemeanors, and traffic matters, as well as all civil cases.[5] The California court system is discussed in more detail in Chapter 5.

Passing a Law in California

In California, a bill may be introduced into either the Senate or the Assembly and may be amended many times as it moves through both Houses. For a bill to be passed, it must receive a majority vote in each of the two houses. After both houses agree on the wording of the bill, it will go to the governor for approval. If the governor approves and signs the act, or if he fails to veto it within seven days, the act will become law. The legislature may, by a two-thirds vote of each house, enact a bill into law over the governor's veto within 60 days. After a bill becomes a statute, it takes effect on January 1st of the following year unless it contains either a clause that specifies a different effective date or a special urgency clause requiring it to go into effect immediately.

In California, laws may also be passed by **initiative**. According the California constitution, "The initiative is the power of the electors to propose statutes and amendments to the Constitution and to adopt or reject them."[4] To use the power of initiative, a petition in favor of the new statute must first be signed by a number of voters equal in number to at least five percent of the votes for all candidates for governor at the last gubernatorial election. The petition is then presented to the Secretary of State, who places the proposed measure on the ballot in the next general election. If it is passed by the voters in a state-wide election, the measure becomes law.

In addition, through a process of **referendum**, California citizens may challenge laws passed by the state legislature. If at least five percent of the people who voted for governor in the last election sign a petition challenging a new law, the law may not go into effect unless it is approved by the voters in a state-wide election.[6]

THE CALIFORNIA PENAL CODE

The California Penal Code is the basic criminal law for the state of California. It was originally enacted in 1872, took effect the following year,[7] and has been modified frequently over the years. The Penal Code originally was based chiefly on the English **common law**, although Spanish law, remnants of California's early domination by Spain and Mexico, also influenced the new legal system. Today, the California legal system is based entirely on written laws. The Penal Code specifically states that no act or omission is a crime or may be punished except as prescribed or authorized by written code or statute.[8] Thus, for a law to be enforced, it must be written down, or codified. There are no common law crimes in California. In addition, a prohibited act is not a crime unless the statute which prohibits the act also provides for a punishment.

Currently, there are three primary sources of criminal law in California, including:

- federal and state constitutions
- statutory law
- case law

Together, the California state constitution and the U.S. Constitution provide the basic framework for criminal law, first by focusing on individual rights and on the limitations placed on government power and second, by requiring the establishment of a judicial system. However, neither constitution significantly emphasizes the creation or definition of crimes.

Statutory law in California may either be passed by the state legislature or by the voters using the power of initiative. Most of the statutes that pertain to crime are found in the Penal Code. However, other state codes, such as the California Vehicle Code, also contain laws which relate to crime and punishment. There are two types of statutes in the Penal Code: **enabling statutes** and **criminal statutes**. Criminal statutes prohibit an act and provide a punishment for violating the statute. Enabling statutes prohibit an act but do not provide a punishment. Because an act is not a crime unless the statute provides a punishment, enabling statutes are considered to be only explanatory in nature.

Case law consists of appellate court decisions or opinions which interpret the meaning of the law. Effectively, case law is made by judges when they hand down decisions in court. Because of the principle of ***stare decisis***, or precedent, a decision made by a judge in one court will be followed by later judges in the state until the same court reverses its decision or until the decision is overturned by a higher court.

The California Penal Code contains two types of statutory criminal law, substantive and procedural. **Substantive criminal laws** are those that define crimes and set forth required punishments. The section of the California Penal Code which defines criminal homicide and outlines the legal punishments which may be imposed by the court is an example of substantive criminal law.[9] **Procedural laws**, on the other hand, focus on the methods that are used to enforce substantive criminal law. In other words, procedural laws outline the rules that the state must follow when dealing with crimes and criminals. These include the procedures that must be used to investigate crimes, arrest suspects, and carry out formal prosecution. The protection against double jeopardy, which is discussed in PC §687, is an example of procedural law.

THE DEFINITION AND CLASSIFICATION OF CRIME

In California, a crime or public offense is defined in PC §15. This statute states that:

> a crime or public offense is an act committed or omitted in violation of a law forbidding or commanding it, and to which is annexed, upon conviction, either of the following punishments:
> (1) Death;
> (2) Imprisonment;
> (3) Fine;
> (4) Removal from office; or
> (5) Disqualification to hold and enjoy any office of honor, trust or profit in this State.

According to PC §16, there are three types of crimes and public offenses: **felonies**, **misdemeanors**, and **infractions**. The difference between the three levels of crimes is not determined by the offense itself, or the action committed by the offender, but by the possible punishment that is prescribed by the Penal Code. Even if the Penal Code does not specifically identify a crime as a misdemeanor or a felony, the classification can easily be inferred from the prescribed sentence.

The three categories of crimes are defined in PC §17. **Felonies** are the most serious crimes in California; a felony is any crime for which the offender may be sentenced to death or to a term of imprisonment in a state prison.[10] Currently, the only felony in California for which an offender may be put to death is first degree murder with special circumstances. A **misdemeanor** is less serious than a felony and is a crime that is punishable by a fine and/or imprisonment in a county jail for not more than one year.[11] Finally, **infractions** are the lowest or least serious category of crime in California and are punishable only by a fine; there is no possibility of a sentence of incarceration either in state prison or a county jail.[12] Many of the offenses listed in the California Vehicle Code, which are punishable only by a traffic ticket, are infractions.

California also has some crimes which are known colloquially as **"wobblers."** Although this term does not actually appear in the Penal Code, it is frequently used in the California courts. A wobbler is a crime that could be either a felony or a misdemeanor, depending on the sentence awarded by the court. For example, PC 461 states that the punishment for second degree burglary is imprisonment in the county jail not exceeding one year or in the state prison. If the offender is sentenced to serve a term in the state prison, the crime is considered to be a felony; if the judge sentences the offender to a term in jail, the crime is considered a misdemeanor. Wobblers are treated as felonies for every purpose until the final judgement by the court.[13] However, if a wobbler is sentenced as a misdemeanor, then from that point on the conviction will be treated as a misdemeanor (for example, for the purposes of any future sentence enhancement).[14]

DEFENSES TO A CRIMINAL CHARGE

There are a wide variety of defenses to a criminal charge. Many are specifically mentioned in the California Penal Code or in other state codes

Justifications

A defendant who uses a **justification** defense admits to the commission of the criminal act but also claims that it was necessary to commit the act in order to avoid some greater evil or harm. Probably the most well-known justification defense is that of **self-defense**, in which the defendant claims that the use of force against the victim was justifiable because it was the only way the defendant could ensure his/her own safety. The issue of **lawful resistence** is discussed primarily in PC §692-694. According to PC §692,

> Lawful resistance to the commission of a public offense may be made:
> 1. By the party about to be injured;
> 2. By other parties.

The following statute (PC §693) outlines the level of resistence that may be used, stating that:

> Resistance sufficient to prevent the offense may be made by the party about to be injured:
> 1. To prevent an offense against his person, or his family, or some member thereof.
> 2. To prevent an illegal attempt by force to take or injure property in his lawful possession.

In addition, PC §694 allows any other person coming to the aid or defense of the person in danger of injury to use the same level of resistence.

It is clear from these statutes that the amount of force used must be proportionate to the amount of force or threat that the defendant is experiencing. Thus, unless the individual about to be injured is in immediate danger of death or great bodily harm, deadly force may not be used. This essentially becomes justifiable homicide. According to PC §197, which discusses the topic of justifiable homicide by private citizens (as opposed to public officers):

> Homicide is ... justifiable when committed by any person in any of the following cases:
> 1. When resisting any attempt to murder any person, or to commit a felony, or to do some great bodily injury upon any person; or,
> 2. When committed in defense of habitation, property, or person, against one who manifestly intends or endeavors, by violence or surprise, to commit a felony, or against one who manifestly intends and endeavors, in a violent, riotous or tumultuous manner, to enter the habitation of another for the purpose of offering violence to any person therein; or,
> 3. When committed in the lawful defense of such person, or of a wife or husband, parent, child, master, mistress, or servant of such person, when there is reasonable ground to apprehend a design to commit a felony or to do some great

bodily injury, and imminent danger of such design being accomplished; but such person, or the person in whose behalf the defense was made, if he was the assailant or engaged in mutual combat, must really and in good faith have endeavored to decline any further struggle before the homicide was committed; or,

4. When necessarily committed in attempting, by lawful ways and means, to apprehend any person for any felony committed, or in lawfully suppressing any riot, or in lawfully keeping and preserving the peace.

It is important to note that simple fear that one of the offenses mentioned in the above statute may be committed is not sufficient to justify the use of deadly force.[15]

Another justification defense is that of **consent**. This defense claims that the injured person voluntarily consented to the actions that caused the injury. It is most commonly used in sex-related offenses, such as rape. PC §261.6 defines consent in the case of sexual offenses as:

> positive cooperation in act or attitude pursuant to an exercise of free will. The person must act freely and voluntarily and have knowledge of the nature of the act or transaction involved.

Consent that is obtained by some form of coercion, such as through the use or threat of force or violence against the victim or another person, does not constitute a defense of consent.[16] However, in cases of statutory rape, a reasonable mistake as to the age of the victim may be an acceptable defense to the crime.[17] The consent defense may also be used in other types of crimes as well. For example, the crime of battery involves the use of force or violence against another person willfully and unlawfully.[18] A battery can be as simple as touching another person against their will. Therefore, a consent defense would contend that the alleged victim consented to the touching.

The defense of **necessity** claims that harm resulting from the illegal act was necessary to prevent some greater harm. The burden of proof is on the defendant to show necessity by a preponderance of the evidence. The necessity defense does not attempt to negate any element of the crime of which the defendant is accused. Instead, the defense says that, because of the circumstances, the defendant should not be punished despite the existence of proof of the crime. For a defense of necessity to be used, the criminal act must have been done to prevent an equal or greater harm and the defendant must have had no viable alternative to committing the crime. Necessity may not be used as a defense if the defendant created the emergency situation that led to the need to commit the crime.

Excuses

A defendant using an **excuse** defense is claiming that at the time of the criminal act some circumstance or personal condition creates a situation under which he/she should not be held criminally accountable. Probably the most well-known (and controversial) defense in this category is that of **insanity**. Although the term insanity is no longer used by mental health professionals, it is a legal term referring to a defense that is based on the defendant's claim that he/she was mentally ill or mentally incapacitated at the time the offense was committed. In California, the burden is on the defendant to prove by a preponderance of evidence that he or she was legally insane at the time of the crime.[19] According to PC §25(b), a person may be found legally insane only if

> the accused person proves by a preponderance of the evidence that he or she was incapable of knowing or understanding the nature and quality of his or her act and of distinguishing right from wrong at the time of the commission of the offense.

Another defense that falls into the category of excuses is that of **involuntary intoxication**. PC §22(a) states that "No act committed by a person while in a state of voluntary intoxication is less criminal by reason of his or her having been in that condition." Voluntary intoxication is defined as "the voluntary ingestion, injection, or taking by any other means of any intoxicating liquor, drug, or other substance."[20] While the Penal Code does not specifically address the issue of involuntary intoxication, it generally is a defense if it can negate the existence of any criminal intent at the time of the crime. Intoxication is only involuntary if the defendant consumed the intoxicating substance unwillingly or unknowingly (for example, if PCP is secretly added to punch at a party).[21]

While in general the old saying that "ignorance of the law is no defense" is true, there are some exceptions in California. According to the Penal Code, **mistake of fact** or **ignorance** may be a defense if it "disproves any criminal intent".[22] For example, mistake of age sometimes may be used as a defense in cases of statutory rape if the defendant can show that the mistake was reasonable.

The defense of **duress** is defined in PC §26 as:

> Persons (unless the crime be punishable with death) who committed the act or made the omission charged under threats or menaces sufficient to show that they had reasonable cause to and did believe their lives would be endangered if they refused.

Essentially, if the defendant commits a crime under some type of threat of imminent death or great bodily harm, he/she is not guilty of the offense. The defendant must have been in immediate danger; a fear of future harm is not sufficient to claim duress. Basically, duress negates the intent required for the crime. The statute provides for one specific exception: duress may not be used as a defense to a crime that is punishable by death.

Procedural Defenses

A **procedural defense** claims that some form of official procedure was not followed or that procedural law was not properly followed during the investigation or the prosecution of the crime.

One procedural defense is the **denial of a speedy trial**. Article I, Section 29 of the California State Constitution states that, "In a criminal case, the people of the State of California have the right to due process of law and to a speedy and public trial." This right is also guaranteed in PC §686. The time limit for a trial to be "speedy" is discussed in PC §1382, and in felony cases is generally 60 days from the date of the defendant's arraignment. The time limit may be extended under certain circumstances. For example, if the defendant requested or consented to an extension or delay of the trial date, he/she may not later claim that the right to a speedy trial was denied.

Another procedural issue is that of **double jeopardy**. Article I, Section 15 of the California State Constitution states that, "Persons may not twice be put in jeopardy for the same offense." Similarly, PC §687 states that

> No person can be subjected to a second prosecution for a public offense for which he has once been prosecuted and convicted or acquitted.

Finally, in the defense of **entrapment**, the defendant claims that the behavior of law enforcement officers induced him/her to commit the illegal act. In California, there are two separate rationales for allowing the use of entrapment as a defense. The first is to prevent the punishment of individuals who would not have violated the law if not for the behavior of law enforcement officials. The second is that the defense acts as a deterrent for police misconduct, working under the belief that it is better to allow some offenders to escape punishment than to allow police officers to behave illegally. The defendant must prove entrapment by a preponderance of the evidence.

The entrapment defense, which is extremely difficult for the defendant to prove, is most commonly used when the defendant was ensnared in an undercover police action; the most frequent use seems to relate to the sale of illegal drugs. In general, the defendant will claim that he/she does not regularly sell drugs but made a sale as a favor to the undercover officer. One of the most common ways for the police to prevent the use of this defense is to make two or more purchases from the same suspect; after the suspect has made multiple sales, the jury is more likely to believe that the undercover officer simply provided the defendant with an opportunity to commit the crime, rather than that the officer induced or encouraged the defendant to engage in a behavior in which he/she would not normally become involved.

SOURCES OF INFORMATION FOR LEGAL RESEARCH

Legal research involves the study of both statutes and case law from court decisions. Because the law is constantly changing, it is essential that only the most recent references be used. Today, much of the material may be found in electronic format: CD-ROMs and on-line computer databases such as WestLaw and LexisNexis have significantly streamlined legal research.

Legal Citations

Decisions of state appellate courts and the U.S. Supreme Court are published in books which are generally known as "reports" or "reporters." A sample case citation is ***People v. McNulty*, 93 Cal. 427**. This particular case stated that an act prohibited by a state statute is not a crime unless the statute also provided a punishment. *People v. McNulty* is the name of the case; all crimes which are heard in California state courts are prosecuted in the name of "The People of the State of California" versus the defendant. The first number (93) represents the volume number in which the case is to be found. "Cal." is an abbreviation for the specific reporter in which the case is to be found (*California Reports*). The second number (427) is the page number of the first page of the reporter on which the decision is found. Therefore, the above citation, 93 Cal. 427, is found beginning on page 427 of volume 93 of the *California Reports*.

Statutory citations resemble case citations. A sample statutory citation is: **PC 187**. PC is an abbreviation for the California Penal Code and 187 refers to the section number of the statute. This particular statute deals with the topic of homicide.

State and federal statutes use the following abbreviations:

- ***United States Code*** (USC) – contains the federal legal code (including the criminal code)
- ***California Penal Code*** (PC) – contains the criminal code of the state of California
- ***California Evidence Code*** (Ev.C.) – contains rules of evidence used in California
- ***California Welfare and Institutions Code*** (W & IC) – includes much of California's juvenile code
- ***California Health and Safety Code*** (H & SC)
- ***California Vehicle Code*** (Veh. C.)

Court decisions are found in the following reporters:

- ***United States Reports*** (US) – contains U.S. Supreme Court decisions
- ***Supreme Court Reporter*** (S.Ct) – contains U.S. Supreme Court decisions
- ***Federal Reporter, 2nd series*** (F.2d) – contains decisions from the Federal Court of Appeals
- ***California Reports*** (C or Cal) – contains decisions from the California Supreme Court (C2d and C3d contain the second and third series of the *California Reports*)
- ***California Appellate Reports*** (CA or Cal. App.) – contains decisions from the California Courts of Appeal (CA 2d, CA 3d, and CA 3d Supp. are continuations of the *California Appellate Reports*)
- ***West's California Reporter*** (Cal.Rptr) – contains decisions from the California Courts of Appeal

Shepard's Citations

Shepard's California Citations, which is available on CD-ROM, contains an analysis of each appellate court decision. Each citation includes a history of the case, other decisions which cite this decision, and any other cases which have modified, overruled, or approved the decision. There are separate analyses for state statutes.

Other Sources of Information

There are a number of other sources of information on Florida law. However, it is important to remember that these sources are not official legal authorities.

A **legal digest** is a research tool that arranges issues by topic for easy reference. It allows a researcher studying a legal point from one case to easily find other court decisions which were made on similar issues. ***West's California Digest*** is one of the most popular legal digests for California. It indexes California's reported cases by both case name and subject.

Black's Law Dictionary is the most popular **legal dictionary** in America today and can be found in any law library. There also are several useful **legal encyclopedias** which discuss California state law and state legal issues. These include ***California Jurisprudence***, Witkin's ***California Crimes***, and Witkin's ***Criminal Procedure***. The Witkin series also includes volumes on California civil law and civil procedure.

Law reviews are journals which contain scholarly legal research articles written by lawyers and law students. All the major law schools in California publish law reviews. Some of the major law reviews available in California include:

- ***Stanford Law Review*** (Stan.L.Rev.)
- ***University of California Law Review*** (Cal.L.Rev.)
- ***University of Southern California Law Review*** (So. Cal. L. Rev.)

Although law reviews are not legal authority, they are cited in the same way as court cases. For example, **30 Cal.L.Rev. 100** would refer to an article beginning on page 100 of volume 30 of the *University of California Law Review.*

NOTES

1. The California State Constitution and the California Statutes may be viewed online by going to the website maintained by the Legislative Council of California (http://www.leginfo.ca.gov/) and selecting the "California Law" tab.
2. California State Constitution, Article 18, Section 1
3. California State Constitution, Article 2, Section 8(b)
4. California State Constitution, Article 2, Section 8(a)
5. California Courts web site (http://www.courtinfo.ca.gov/courts/trial/about.htm)
6. California State Constitution, Article 2, Section 9
7. PC §2
8. PC §6
9. Penal Code, Part 1, Title 8, Chapter 1
10. PC §17(a)
11. PC §19
12. PC §19.6
13. *US v. Robinson*, 967 F.2d 287, 293 (9th Cir.1992)
14. *People v. Marshall*, 227 Cal.App.3d 502, 504, 277 Cal.Rptr. 846 (1991)
15. PC §198
16. PC §261(a)(2)
17. *People v. Winters* (1996) 242 Cal.App.2d 711, 716, 51 Cal.Rptr. 735; *People v. Hernandez* (1964) 61 Cal.2d 529, 534, 39 Cal.Rptr. 361, 393 P.2d 673.
18. PC §242
19. Evidence Code §522
20. PC §22(c)
21. *People v. Scott* (1983) 146 Cal.App.3d 823, 826-887, 194 Cal.Rptr. 633
22. PC §26

CHAPTER 3

INDEX CRIMES

INTRODUCTION

The Federal Bureau of Investigation annually publishes the ***Uniform Crime Reports***[1] (UCR), the most widely used source of official data on crime and criminals in the United States. Much of the UCR deals with **index crimes**, a set of eight serious offenses that the FBI uses as a measure of crime in the United States. These are also known as **Part I Offenses** and include four violent crimes and four property crimes. The eight index crimes measured by the FBI are:

- homicide
- forcible rape
- robbery
- aggravated assault
- burglary
- larceny-theft
- motor-vehicle theft
- arson

However, the definitions used by the FBI in compiling the UCR are not always the same as those found in the California Penal Code. This chapter will discuss the definitions of these eight serious crimes as provided by California state statutes.

CRIMINAL HOMICIDE

Homicide is the killing of one human being by another. If that killing is illegal, then it is a form of **criminal homicide**. In California, criminal homicides are divided into two types: murder and manslaughter. Murder includes both first degree and second degree murder while manslaughter encompasses voluntary, involuntary, and vehicular manslaughter.

In addition, California recognizes several categories of non-criminal homicide, including justifiable homicide and excusable homicide.

Murder

PC 187 (a) defines **murder** as "the unlawful killing of a human being, or a fetus, with malice aforethought." The statute does include some exceptions relating to the legal use of abortion. The two categories of murder recognized in California, first degree murder and second degree murder, are more specifically defined in PC §189, which states that:

> All murder which is perpetrated by means of a destructive device or explosive, a weapon of mass destruction, knowing use of ammunition designed primarily to penetrate metal or armor, poison, lying in wait, torture, or by any other kind of willful, deliberate, and premeditated killing, or which is committed in the perpetration of, or attempt to perpetrate, arson, rape, carjacking, robbery, burglary, mayhem, kidnapping, train wrecking, or any act punishable under Section 206 [torture], 286 [forced sodomy], 288 [child sexual molestation], 288a [forced oral copulation], or 289 [rape or sodomy with a foreign object], or any murder which is perpetrated by means of discharging a firearm from a motor vehicle, intentionally at another person outside of the vehicle with the intent to inflict death, is murder of the first degree. All other kinds of murders are of the second degree ... To prove the killing was "deliberate and premeditated," it shall not be necessary to prove the defendant maturely and meaningfully reflected upon the gravity of his or her act.

Essentially, this statute divides **first degree murder** into three types. The first is **deliberate or premeditated murder**. This type of murder requires more than simple intent; "deliberate" means that the offender carefully considered his or her course of action and "premeditated" means that the offender thought the murder over in advance. This category does not require the offender intended to kill a specific person. However, if the offender intends to kill one person and accidently kills another by mistake, the required intent for first degree murder is still present. The second type of first degree murder defined in PC §189 is **statutory first degree murder**. This category includes any murder committed by one of the specific means listed in the statute (a destructive device or explosive, a weapon of mass destruction, poison, armor-piercing ammunition, etc.) Finally, **first degree felony murder** occurs when murder is committed during the commission or attempted commission of one of the thirteen felonies specifically listed in PC §189 (arson, rape, carjacking, robbery, burglary, mayhem, kidnapping, train wrecking, torture, forced sodomy, sexual molestation of a child, forced oral copulation, and rape or sodomy with a foreign object). This type of first degree murder does not require deliberation or premeditation. It merely requires that the offender was engaged in one of the crimes listed in the statute and that death occurred as a consequence of, and while the offender was committing (or attempting to commit), that crime. Even if the death occurred due to negligence, recklessness, or accident, the defendant may still be convicted of first degree murder. However, if the death occurred while the offender was engaged in the commission of a crime that is not specifically listed in PC §189, then the offender is not guilty of felony murder in the first degree, although he/she may be guilty of a lower degree of felony murder.

According to PC §189, any murder that is not one of those specified as first degree murder is a **murder in the second degree**. This includes any unlawful killing of a human being resulting from an intentional act, or from an act that has natural consequences that are inherently dangerous, or from a dangerous act deliberately performed with conscious disregard for human life. It also includes second-degree felony murder. While malice aforethought is required for all types of second degree murder except felony murder, deliberation and premeditation are not required. **Second**

degree felony murder occurs when murder is committed during a felony that is not listed in PC §189 and that is inherently dangerous to human life.

The legal punishments for first and second degree murder are discussed in PC §190. First degree murder is punishable by death, imprisonment in the state prison for life without the possibility of parole, or imprisonment in the state prison for a term of 25 years to life."[2] The penalty is limited to death or life imprisonment without possibility of parole only if the crime involved one of 22 special circumstances listed in PC §190.2. PC §190.1 discusses the proceedings for determining the sentence in the case of first degree murder. The process involves two separate phases. The first phase involves the determination of guilt of the crime of first degree murder, and the determination of the existence of at least one of the special circumstances outlined in PC §190.2. The second phase involves a determination of the sentence: death or life imprisonment without parole.

Capital punishment in California is discussed in more detail in Chapter 7.

The penalty for second degree murder is "imprisonment in the state prison for a term of 15 years to life."[3] The statute lists several exceptions to this penalty. For example, according to PC §190(c),

> Every person guilty of murder in the second degree shall be punished by imprisonment in the state prison for a term of life without the possibility of parole if the victim was a peace officer ... who was killed while engaged in the performance of his or her duties, and the defendant knew, or reasonably should have known, that the victim was a peace officer engaged in the performance of his or her duties, and any of the following facts has been charged and found true:
> (1) The defendant specifically intended to kill the peace officer.
> (2) The defendant specifically intended to inflict great bodily injury ... on a peace officer.
> (3) The defendant personally used a dangerous or deadly weapon in the commission of the offense...
> (4) The defendant personally used a firearm in the commission of the offense...

There are a number of other statutory circumstances that also increase the punishment for second degree murder.[4]

Manslaughter

PC §192 defines **manslaughter** as "the unlawful killing of a human being without malice." The statute recognizes three basic types of manslaughter, which are listed in the statute. **Voluntary manslaughter** is the unlawful killing of a human being without malice but in the heat of passion or during a sudden quarrel. The absence of malice is what differentiates this crime from murder. In addition, there may be no "cooling off" period between the quarrel or event that caused the heat of passion and the actual killing. If there is a reasonable cooling off period between the act or event causing the heat of passion and the killing, the crime may become premeditated murder.

Involuntary manslaughter is manslaughter that occurs

> in the commission of an unlawful act, not amounting to felony; or in the commission of a lawful act which might produce death, in an unlawful manner, or without due caution and circumspection. This subdivision shall not apply to acts committed in the driving of a vehicle.[5]

The key difference between voluntary and involuntary manslaughter is that involuntary manslaughter does not require any intent to kill. There are three main ways in which involuntary manslaughter may be committed. The first involves a homicide that occurs during the commission of a misdemeanor, such as a death occurring during a simple assault or battery.[6] The second type of involuntary manslaughter involves a defendant who engages in a lawful act in an unlawful manner; for example, a death resulting from a medical procedure that was not performed with adequate caution and care.[7] The third type occurs when the defendant, through criminal negligence, allows someone in his or her custody or care to die from lack of medical care and attention.

Finally, **vehicular manslaughter** is the unlawful killing of a human being, unintentionally and without malice, while driving a vehicle. There are four basic types of vehicular manslaughter. All four have three elements in common. They all involve the unlawful killing of a human without malice aforethought, they all occur while the defendant is driving a vehicle, and they all occur in the commission of an unlawful act that is not a felony or in the commission of a lawful act that might produce death in an unlawful manner.[8] In addition to these three common elements, each of the four types of vehicular manslaughter has a fourth element that is unique. The first type of vehicular manslaughter involves death that is due to the gross negligence of the driver.[9] The second involves death due to the negligence (but not gross negligence) of the driver.[10] The third involves death due to the driver's negligence while the driver is under the influence of alcohol or drugs.[11] Finally, the fourth type involves vehicular manslaughter knowingly committed for financial gain.[12] In addition, PC §191.5 discusses the crime of **gross vehicular manslaughter while intoxicated**, which involves death due to the gross negligence of the driver while the driver is under the influence of drugs or alcohol.

The legal punishments for manslaughter are outlined in PC §193. The punishment for voluntary manslaughter is imprisonment in the state prison for three, six, or eleven years. The punishment for involuntary manslaughter is imprisonment in the state prison for two, three, or four years. The punishment for vehicular manslaughter varies by type but ranges from imprisonment in the county jail for up to one year to imprisonment in the state prison for as much as ten years.

Non-Criminal Homicide

Although the UCR focuses specifically on criminal homicide, there are situations when the killing of one human being by another is lawful and therefore not a crime. Non-criminal homicides may be justifiable or excusable.

Excusable homicide is a death that is caused by an accident or other misfortune, when no unlawful intent is involved in the act that caused the death. PC §195 defines excusable homicide, stating that:

> Homicide is excusable in the following cases:
> 1. When committed by accident and misfortune, or in doing any other lawful act by lawful means, with usual and ordinary caution, and without any unlawful intent.
> 2. When committed by accident and misfortune, in the heat of passion, upon any sudden and sufficient provocation, or upon a sudden combat, when no undue advantage is taken, nor any dangerous weapon used, and when the killing is not done in a cruel or unusual manner.

An automobile accident that does not involve negligence or any unlawful act on the part of the driver is an example of excusable homicide.

In California, **justifiable homicide** is a killing to protect society. A justifiable homicide may be committed either by police officers in the performance of their duties or by other members of society. Justifiable homicide by a peace officer is defined in PC §196 as:

> Homicide is justifiable when committed by public officers and those acting by their command in their aid and assistance, either—
> 1. In obedience to any judgment of a competent Court; or,
> 2. When necessarily committed in overcoming actual resistance to the execution of some legal process, or in the discharge of any other legal duty; or,
> 3. When necessarily committed in retaking felons who have been rescued or have escaped, or when necessarily committed in arresting persons charged with felony, and who are fleeing from justice or resisting such arrest.

Justifiable homicide committed by an individual who is not a police officer is defined in PC §197 as:

> Homicide is also justifiable when committed by any person in any of the following cases:
> 1. When resisting any attempt to murder any person, or to commit a felony, or to do some great bodily injury upon any person; or,
> 2. When committed in defense of habitation, property, or person, against one who manifestly intends or endeavors, by violence or surprise, to commit a felony, or against one who manifestly intends and endeavors, in a violent, riotous or tumultuous manner, to enter the habitation of another for the purpose of offering violence to any person therein; or,
> 3. When committed in the lawful defense of such person, or of a wife or husband, parent, child, master, mistress, or servant of such person, when there is reasonable ground to apprehend a design to commit a

felony or to do some great bodily injury, and imminent danger of such design being accomplished; but such person, or the person in whose behalf the defense was made, if he was the assailant or engaged in mutual combat, must really and in good faith have endeavored to decline any further struggle before the homicide was committed; or,

4. When necessarily committed in attempting, by lawful ways and means, to apprehend any person for any felony committed, or in lawfully suppressing any riot, or in lawfully keeping and preserving the peace.

There are no punishments associated with justifiable or excusable homicides as they are not forms of criminal homicide. If a homicide is ruled justifiable or excusable, the defendant at trial must be acquitted and released.[13]

FORCIBLE RAPE

In the Uniform Crime Reporting Program, **forcible rape** is defined as "the carnal knowledge of a female forcibly and against her will."[14] However, in California, the definition of rape is gender-neutral; it does not specify the gender of the victim. Therefore, in California, a woman may be convicted of raping a man. PC §261(a) outlines the acts that constitute the crime of rape in California:

> Rape is an act of sexual intercourse accomplished with a person not the spouse of the perpetrator, under any of the following circumstances:
>
> (1) Where a person is incapable, because of a mental disorder or developmental or physical disability, of giving legal consent, and this is known or reasonably should be known to the person committing the act...
>
> (2) Where it is accomplished against a person's will by means of force, violence, duress, menace, or fear of immediate and unlawful bodily injury on the person or another.
>
> (3) Where a person is prevented from resisting by any intoxicating or anesthetic substance, or any controlled substance, and this condition was known, or reasonably should have been known by the accused.
>
> (4) Where a person is at the time unconscious of the nature of thc act, and this is known to the accused...
>
> (5) Where a person submits under the belief that the person committing the act is the victim's spouse, and this belief is induced by any artifice, pretense, or concealment practiced by the accused, with intent to induce the belief.
>
> (6) Where the act is accomplished against the victim's will by threatening to retaliate in the future against the victim or any other person, and there is a reasonable possibility that the perpetrator will execute the threat...

> (7) Where the act is accomplished against the victim's will by threatening to use the authority of a public official to incarcerate, arrest, or deport the victim or another, and the victim has a reasonable belief that the perpetrator is a public official...

According to California law, "any sexual penetration, however slight, is sufficient to complete the crime."[15]

In addition to the basic crime of rape of a non-spouse, California also recognizes several other types of rape. **Forcible rape in concert** occurs when several individuals work together to forcibly rape a victim. A defendant does not have to actually physically take part in the rape to be convicted of this crime; he/she may simply have aided and abetted the actual perpetrator.[16] Because PC §261 includes a marital exemption for the crime of rape, the crime of **rape of a spouse** was added to the penal code in 1974. According to PC §262(a), spousal rape may occur under any of the following circumstances:

> Rape of a person who is the spouse of the perpetrator is an act of sexual intercourse accomplished under any of the following circumstances:
> (1) Where it is accomplished against a person's will by means of force, violence, duress, menace, or fear of immediate and unlawful bodily injury on the person or another.
> (2) Where a person is prevented from resisting by any intoxicating or anesthetic substance, or any controlled substance, and this condition was known, or reasonably should have been known, by the accused.
> (3) Where a person is at the time unconscious of the nature of the act, and this is known to the accused...
> (4) Where the act is accomplished against the victim's will by threatening to retaliate in the future against the victim or any other person, and there is a reasonable possibility that the perpetrator will execute the threat...
> (5) Where the act is accomplished against the victim's will by threatening to use the authority of a public official to incarcerate, arrest, or deport the victim or another, and the victim has a reasonable belief that the perpetrator is a public official...

Finally, **statutory rape** involves sexual intercourse with a minor (a person under the age of 18) who is not the spouse of the perpetrator.[17] The seriousness of this type of rape varies depending on the age of the victim and the perpetrator. For example, if the minor is no more than three years younger or older than the perpetrator, the crime is considered to be a misdemeanor.[18] If the perpetrator is more than three years older than the minor, or if the perpetrator is at least 21 years of age and the victim is less than 16 years of age, the crime may be either a misdemeanor or a felony.[19] The statute also outlines the various punishments for statutory rape.

A key element of the crime of rape (with the exception of statutory rape) is the victim's lack of consent. Consent is defined as:

> positive cooperation in act or attitude pursuant to an exercise of free will. The person must act freely and voluntarily and have knowledge of the nature of the act or transaction involved. A current or previous dating or marital relationship shall not be sufficient to constitute consent where consent is at issue...[20]

There are a number of ways in which lack of consent on the part of the victim can be established. For example, if the defendant used or threatened to use force, the victim may be considered unable to consent. It is not necessary for the victim to resist physically for the act to be a crime. In addition, the victim's request that the defender use some sort of birth control device (such as a condom) is not alone sufficient to constitute consent.[21] Similarly, lack of consent may be established if the victim was placed in fear of some future retaliation, if the victim's consent was obtained through fraud, if the victim was unable to consent or resist due to intoxication from drugs or alcohol, if the victim is unconscious, or if the victim has a mental, physical, or developmental disability making him or her unable to consent legally.

The punishments for forcible and spousal rape are set out in PC §264. Both crimes are "punishable by imprisonment in the state prison for three, six, or eight years." In addition, rape in concert may be punishable by imprisonment in the state prison for five, seven, or nine years.[22]

ROBBERY

PC §211 defines **robbery** as:

> the felonious taking of personal property in the possession of another, from his person or immediate presence, and against his will, accomplished by means of force or fear.

This definition includes elements of both larceny-theft and assault, because it involves taking personal property but also involves the use of force or fear against the victim to illegally acquire this property. This element of force is what distinguishes robbery from larceny. Because of the use of force or fear to illegally acquire personal property, California considers robbery to be both a crime against the person and a crime against property. Unlike in the case of a larceny, the type or the value of the property taken in a robbery is irrelevant. In addition, a defendant may be found guilty of robbery even if the property taken was illegal contraband (for example, illegal drugs).[23]

The use of force or fear is an essential element of the crime of robbery, although actual force is not required. A threat that places the victim in fear is sufficient. Either force or fear is sufficient to meet the requirement outlined in the definition; it is not necessary for the prosecution to prove the existence of both to meet this requirement. The element of fear in the crime of robbery is defined in PC §212 as either:

> 1. The fear of an unlawful injury to the person or property of the person robbed, or of any relative of his or member of his family; or,

2. The fear of an immediate and unlawful injury to the person or property of anyone in the company of the person robbed at the time of the robbery.

Force is not specifically defined in the Penal Code but the courts have held that the amount of force used must be greater than that necessary to simply seize the property from the victim, or the crime will be considered a "theft from a person" rather than a robbery. For example, just snatching or grabbing an item such as a purse from the victim's hands may not meet the definition of robbery in California.[24]

Because the felonious taking of property is also a requirement for the crime of robbery, if no property is actually taken, the defendant cannot be found guilty of robbery. However, he/she may be guilty of assault, battery, or some other crime.

California recognizes **first degree robbery** and **second degree robbery**. A list of those crimes constituting first degree robbery appears in PC §212.5 and includes:

- the robbery of a person performing his or her duties as the operator of a vehicle for hire (bus, taxicab, cable car, etc.)
- the robbery of a passenger of such a vehicle
- all robberies committed in an inhabited building or dwelling structure
- the robbery of a person who is using an ATM
- all robberies which occur immediately after a person has used an ATM and while the victim is still in the vicinity of the ATM

All other robberies are second degree robberies. It is clear from PC §212.5 that the distinction between first degree and second degree robbery is not based on the type of weapon used or the amount or value of the property taken but rather upon where the robbery occurred. Robberies that occur in locations where the victim is especially vulnerable (on public transportation, in a dwelling, at an ATM) are considered to be more serious than those committed in other locations.

The punishments for robbery are outlined in PC §213. Both first and second degree robbery are felonies in California. In most cases, robbery is punishable by imprisonment in the state prison for three, four, or six years. Robbery of an inhabited dwelling that is committed in concert is punishable by imprisonment in the state prison for three, six, or nine years. The punishment for second degree robbery is imprisonment in the state prison for two, three, or five years.

Recently, California codified the crime of **carjacking,** which is a form of robbery. PC §215(a) defines carjacking as:

> the felonious taking of a motor vehicle in the possession of another, from his or her person or immediate presence, or from the person or immediate presence of a passenger of the motor vehicle, against his or her will and with the intent to either permanently or temporarily deprive the person in possession of the motor vehicle of his or her possession, accomplished by means of force or fear.

Essentially, carjacking involves robbing the victim of a motor vehicle. The victim does not need to be the owner of the vehicle, only to have custody of the vehicle or to be a passenger in the vehicle at the time of the crime. The requirements regarding force and fear are the same as for any other robbery. Even if the only individual in the vehicle at the time of the crime is an infant or child too young to be able to consent to the taking of the vehicle, the courts have held that the defendant may be convicted of carjacking.[25] The punishment for carjacking in California is imprisonment in the state prison for three, five, or nine years.

ASSAULT AND BATTERY

There is often some confusion about the actual meaning of **assault**. Although many people believe that assault involves inflicting an injury upon another person, this is not always the case. In many states, including California, an assault is an intentional attempt or threat to cause injury. If the injury is actually inflicted, a **battery** has occurred. The Uniform Crime Reporting Program focuses specifically on aggravated assault, which it defines as:

> an unlawful attack by one person upon another for the purpose of inflicting severe or aggravated bodily injury. This type of assault is usually accompanied by the use of a weapon or by means likely to produce death or great bodily harm.[26]

In California, PC §240 defines an assault as "an unlawful attempt, coupled with a present ability, to commit a violent injury on the person of another." Effectively, an assault is an attempted battery. There is no crime of attempted assault in California.

A key element of an assault is the unlawful nature of the attempt to commit a violent injury. Therefore, an attempt to injure that is carried out in self defense is not a criminal assault. In addition, if the act is made with the consent of the victim (for example, during a sporting event such as a boxing or wrestling match), then it may not be an assault. Another important element of assault is intent. Because of this, it is not possible in California to commit an accidental or unintentional assault.

Assault as defined in PC §240 is a misdemeanor and is punishable by a fine of up to $1,000 or by imprisonment in the county jail for up to six months, or both.[27] However, the punishment is increased under certain circumstances, generally relating to the victim or the location of the crime. For example, if the victim of the assault is a peace officer, firefighter, emergency medical technician, mobile intensive care paramedic, lifeguard, process server, traffic officer, or animal control officer engaged in the performance of his or her duties, or a physician or nurse engaged in rendering emergency medical care outside a health care facility, and the defendant reasonably should know the victim's status, the maximum possible fine is increased to $2,000 and the maximum term of imprisonment to one year.[28] Other situations that may increase the penalty for the crime include assault committed on school or park property, [29] an assault committed against a victim on public transportation,[30] or an assault committed against a school employee engaged in the performance of his or her duties, or in retaliation for some official action.[31]

Battery is defined in PC §242 as the "wilful and unlawful use of force or violence upon the person of another." The level of force required to satisfy this definition is very small and the actual infliction of bodily harm is not required. Merely touching the victim is enough, even if it does not cause any physical injury. It is not possible to commit a battery without touching the victim in some way, although the touching could be indirect (e.g., throwing something in the victim's face). Assault is a key element of the crime of battery, so it is not possible to convict a defendant of both crimes. Battery as defined in PC §242 is a misdemeanor and is punishable by a fine of up to $2,000 or imprisonment in a county jail for up to six months, or both.[32] As with the crime of assault, the punishment for battery may be increased under certain conditions.[33]

The California Penal Code does not recognize the crime of aggravated assault, which is one of the Part I crimes included in the *Uniform Crime Reports*. However, there are several crimes mentioned in the Penal Code which fit the basic definition. PC §243(d) discusses the crime of **battery with serious bodily injury**. This crime is a wobbler as it is punishable by imprisonment in a county jail for up to one year or by imprisonment in the state prison for two, three, or four years. PC §220 outlines another type of felony assault, stating that "every person who assaults another with intent to commit mayhem, rape, sodomy, oral copulation..." or a variety of other sexual offenses may be punished by imprisonment in the state prison for two, four, or six years. PC §245 discusses **assault with a deadly weapon**, which is another form of aggravated assault. The statute is extremely complex because the punishment varies depending on a variety of factors, including the type of weapon used (firearm versus other deadly weapons) and whether the victim was a peace officer engaged in the performance of his or her duties. PC §245 states that:

> (a)
> (1) Any person who commits an assault upon the person of another with a deadly weapon or instrument other than a firearm or by any means of force likely to produce great bodily injury shall be punished by imprisonment in the state prison for two, three, or four years, or in a county jail for not exceeding one year, or by a fine not exceeding ten thousand dollars ($10,000), or by both the fine and imprisonment.
> (2) Any person who commits an assault upon the person of another with a firearm shall be punished by imprisonment in the state prison for two, three, or four years, or in a county jail for not less than six months and not exceeding one year, or by both a fine not exceeding ten thousand dollars ($10,000) and imprisonment.
> (3) Any person who commits an assault upon the person of another with a machinegun ... or an assault weapon ... shall be punished by imprisonment in the state prison for 4, 8, or 12 years.
>
> (b) Any person who commits an assault upon the person of another with a semiautomatic firearm shall be punished by imprisonment in the state prison for three, six, or nine years.

(c) Any person who commits an assault with a deadly weapon or instrument, other than a firearm, or by any means likely to produce great bodily injury upon the person of a peace officer or firefighter, and who knows or reasonably should know that the victim is a peace officer or firefighter engaged in the performance of his or her duties, when the peace officer or firefighter is engaged in the performance of his or her duties, shall be punished by imprisonment in the state prison for three, four, or five years.

(d)

(1) Any person who commits an assault with a firearm upon the person of a peace officer or firefighter, and who knows or reasonably should know that the victim is a peace officer or firefighter engaged in the performance of his or her duties, when the peace officer or firefighter is engaged in the performance of his or her duties, shall be punished by imprisonment in the state prison for four, six, or eight years.

(2) Any person who commits an assault upon the person of a peace officer or firefighter with a semiautomatic firearm and who knows or reasonably should know that the victim is a peace officer or firefighter engaged in the performance of his or her duties, when the peace officer or firefighter is engaged in the performance of his or her duties, shall be punished by imprisonment in the state prison for five, seven, or nine years.

(3) Any person who commits an assault with a machinegun ... or an assault weapon ... upon the person of a peace officer or firefighter, and who knows or reasonably should know that the victim is a peace officer or firefighter engaged in the performance of his or her duties, shall be punished by imprisonment in the state prison for 6, 9, or 12 years.

California also recognizes the crime of **sexual battery**, which is distinct from the crime of rape. Sexual battery is committed if the offender

> touches an intimate part of another person while that person is unlawfully restrained by the accused or an accomplice, and if the touching is against the will of the person touched and is for the purpose of sexual arousal, sexual gratification, or sexual abuse....[34]

Sexual battery is a wobbler. The punishment for this crime is either imprisonment in a county jail for up to one year and a fine of up to $2,000 or imprisonment in the state prison for two, three, or four years, and a fine of up to $10,000.[35] The punishment is increased if the victim is institutionalized for medical treatment and is seriously disabled or medically incapacitated,[36] if the victim is an employee of the defendant,[37] or if the victim is a minor.

BURGLARY

The original statute defining **burglary** in California was enacted in 1872 and specified that the crime must occur at night, must involve forcible breaking and entering or illegal entry, must be of a dwelling or vessel, and must involve the intent to commit larceny or any felony.[39] This definition mirrored that found in common law, which defined burglary as the breaking and entering of a dwelling at night with intent to commit a felony. Today, the definition of burglary includes structures other than a dwelling place, can occur during the daytime as well as at night, and can involve either an intended felony or misdemeanor. The UCR defines burglary simply as the "unlawful entry of a structure to commit a felony or theft."[49]

In California, the current definition of burglary is found in PC §459, which states that

> Every person who enters any house, room, apartment, tenement, shop, warehouse, store, mill, barn, stable, outhouse or other building, tent, vessel,... floating home,... railroad car, locked or sealed cargo container, whether or not mounted on a vehicle, trailer coach,... any house car,...inhabited camper,... vehicle... when the doors are locked, aircraft,... or mine or any underground portion thereof, with intent to commit grand or petit larceny or any felony is guilty of burglary. As used in this chapter, "inhabited" means currently being used for dwelling purposes, whether occupied or not.

Essentially, a burglary occurs when an offender enters one of the structures listed in the statute with felonious intent. Forcible entry, or "breaking", is not required to meet the entry element of the statute. The California courts have held that any type of entry is enough to constitute the crime of burglary, even if it is only a portion of the defendant's body. If the defendant extended any part of his or her body far enough into the location to commit the intended offense, breaking the airspace of the location, the entry element of the crime is considered to have been met. In one case, the courts held that a defendant who merely reached through an open window was guilty of burglary.[41] However, if an item falls out of the window and is picked up from the street by an individual who did not actually enter the window, the element of entry is not met and the individual is not guilty of the crime of burglary.

The elimination of the requirement of "breaking" from the common law definition also means that it is possible for a burglary to occur even if the victim invited the defendant into the structure or in some other way gave the offender permission to enter. The permission to enter is canceled or nullified by the criminal intent of the burglar. Therefore, if an invited guest enters a home, steals property belonging to the host, and then leaves, he/she could be convicted of burglary. Similarly, if an individual enters a structure at a time when it was open to the public (for example, entering a shop during regular business hours) but remains within after he/she knew that the premises were closed to the public, the defendant may be guilty of burglary. In addition, if the defendant is in a location that is open to the public but enters or remains in areas of that location that he/she knew or should have known were not open to the public, he/she may be guilty of burglary. However, an individual cannot be found guilty of burglarizing his or her own property, as he/she has the legal right to enter the premises. The one exception to this is vehicular burglary; the statute states that the doors of the vehicle must be locked. Therefore, an automobile is not subject to burglary if the doors are not locked or if the windows are left rolled down.

In California, the crime of burglary is completed when the offender enters the building with larcenous or felonious intent, regardless of whether the intended larceny or felony is actually committed. The item of property intended to be taken must have at least some minimal intrinsic value. In one case, a defendant entered a dwelling intending to take a shower. Because this would have involved the taking of a small amount of property (water, soap, and shampoo), he was convicted of burglary.[42]

California recognizes both first and second degree burglary. According to PC §460,

> (a) Every burglary of an inhabited dwelling house, vessel ... which is inhabited and designed for habitation, floating home ... or trailer coach ... or the inhabited portion of any other building, is burglary of the first degree.
> (b) All other kinds of burglary are of the second degree.

First degree burglary is punishable by imprisonment in the state prison for two, four, or six years. Second degree burglary is a wobbler because it is punishable by imprisonment in a county jail for up to one year, or in the state prison.[43]

There are actually several exceptions to the statement in PC §460(b) above. One is burglary with the use of an acetylene torch or explosive. PC §464 outlines a separate punishment schedule for this crime, which is a felony. In addition, PC §463 discusses the crime of looting during a state of emergency or during a local emergency.

LARCENY-THEFT

The FBI defines larceny-theft as:

> the unlawful taking, carrying, leading, or riding away of property from the possession or constructive possession of another. It includes crimes such as shoplifting, pocket-picking, purse-snatching, thefts from motor vehicles, thefts of motor vehicle parts and accessories, bicycle thefts, etc., in which no use of force, violence, or fraud occurs.[44]

The present California statutes relating to **theft** have merged a number of offenses, including larceny, larceny by trick, embezzlement, and obtaining property by false pretenses into one "theft" statute. PC §490a states that:

> Wherever any law or statute of this state refers to or mentions larceny, embezzlement, or stealing, said law or statute shall hereafter be read and interpreted as if the word "theft" were substituted therefor.

The California Penal Code defines theft as:

> Every person who shall feloniously steal, take, carry, lead, or drive away the personal property of another, or who shall fraudulently appropriate property which has been entrusted to him or her, or who shall knowingly and designedly, by any false or fraudulent representation or pretense, defraud any other person of money, labor or real or personal property, or who causes or procures others to report falsely of his or her wealth or mercantile character and by thus imposing upon any person, obtains credit and thereby fraudulently gets or obtains possession of money, or property or obtains the labor or service of another, is guilty of theft.[45]

Thus essentially theft involves the intentional taking and carrying away the personal property of another person. There are four main elements of the crime of theft in California. The first element is that the stolen property must be taken without the owner's consent or against the owner's will. It is not necessary for the taking to involve actual force or even fear; the offender may obtain possession of the property through fraud or trickery. The second element of the crime of theft is that the stolen item must be the personal property of another person. An individual cannot be convicted of stealing his or her own property unless someone else has a greater right of possession or ownership. For example, a husband cannot charge his wife with theft of property which they own jointly. However, the victim does not have to be the actual owner of the property, he or she only needs to possess it at the time of the crime. Thus, it is possible for a thief to be the victim of a theft.[46] In addition, it is possible to convict a defendant of the crime of theft even if the personal property stolen is something that is unlawful to possess (for example, illegal drugs).

The third element is **asportation**, which is the act of taking physical possession of and carrying away or moving the property. For the crime of theft to be completed, the thief must not only take possession of the property being stolen but also carry it away. Even if the property is returned to its original location before the owner realizes it has been stolen, the offender may still be convicted of theft. The amount of movement does not have to be very great. In one early case, a defendant who attempted to steal a coat that was chained to a store dummy was convicted of theft even though the individual was unable to actually remove the coat from the store premises.[47] Finally, the fourth element involves intent. The defendant must, at the time of the theft, have had specific intent to permanently deprive the owner of the property being taken. If the intent is not formed until after the property was taken, the crime is not theft, although the individual may be convicted of some other offense, such as embezzlement. If an individual takes property for temporary use only, and with the intention of returning it to the proper owner (for example, borrowing an item without the owner's permission), he or she has not committed a theft.

According to PC §486, California recognizes two classifications of theft: grant theft and petty theft. **Grand theft**, which is defined in PC §487, mainly consists of unlawfully taking money, labor, or property (real or personal) which has a value of more than $400. In addition, the statute lists several situations in which taking of property valued at less than this amount is considered to be a grand theft. These include:

- the theft of certain farm crops or domestic fowls with a value of over $100
- the theft of certain aquacultural products, from a commercial or research operation, with a value of over $100
- the theft of money, labor, or property from one's employer when the value of the property taken over any twelve-month period is at least $400
- any theft of any amount from a person
- the theft of a firearm, regardless of the value of the item
- the theft of an automobile or certain farm animals

PC §488 states that any theft not classified as a grand theft is a **petty theft**.

The punishment for grand theft is outlined in PC §489, which states that unless the crime involves the theft of a firearm, the punishment for grand theft is imprisonment in a county jail for up to one year or in the state prison. Grand theft of a firearm is punishable by imprisonment in the state prison for 16 months, two, or three years. Grand theft is a wobbler because it may be punishable either as a felony or as a misdemeanor. Petty theft is always a misdemeanor. PC §490 states that "Petty theft is punishable by fine not exceeding one thousand dollars ..., or by imprisonment in the county jail not exceeding six months, or both."

MOTOR VEHICLE THEFT

The UCR considers **motor vehicle theft** to be a separate index crime from larceny-theft. It is defined by the FBI as:

> the theft or attempted theft of a motor vehicle, this offense category includes the stealing of automobiles, trucks, buses, motorcycles, motorscooters, snowmobiles, etc.[48]

While California does not consider motor vehicle theft to be a separate crime category, there are several crimes outlined in the Penal Code which do correspond to this index crime. The statutory definition of **grand theft** (PC 487(d)) includes the theft of an automobile. However, it is necessary to prove that the offender intended to permanently defraud the owner of the property to convict an offender of grand theft under this statute and it may be difficult to prove such intent. In addition, **carjacking** is defined in PC §215(a) and does involve the taking of a motor vehicle from the person or custody of another person. However, because of the use of force involved, the California Penal Code considers carjacking to be a form of robbery rather than a theft.

PC §499b discusses the crime of **joy-riding**, which involves taking a vehicle without the owner's permission "for the purpose of temporarily using or operating the same." This crime is a misdemeanor and is punishable by a fine of up to $400, or by imprisonment of up to three months, or by both the fine and imprisonment.

Finally, the California Vehicle Code also includes a vehicle theft statute. Veh.C. 10851(a) states that:

> Any person who drives or takes a vehicle not his or her own, without the consent of the owner thereof, and with intent either to permanently or temporarily deprive the owner thereof of his or her title to or possession of the vehicle, whether with or without intent to steal the vehicle, or any person who is a party or an accessory to or an accomplice in the driving or unauthorized taking or stealing, is guilty of a public offense...

This crime is a wobbler; it is punishable by imprisonment in a county jail for up to one year or in the state prison, or by a fine of up to $5,000, or by both the fine and imprisonment.

ARSON

Like burglary, the common-law felony crime of **arson** was a crime specifically against the dwelling of another person. While it could occur at any time of day, nighttime arson was considered to be a more serious crime. However, by 1929, the scope of the crime had been significantly expanded to include the burning of a wide variety of types of property and the definition of the crime has been revised and expanded several more times since then.

The UCR defines arson as:

> any willful or malicious burning or attempt to burn, with or without intent to defraud, a dwelling house, public building, motor vehicle or aircraft, personal property of another, etc.[49]

Today, the California Penal Code states that,

> A person is guilty of arson when he or she willfully and maliciously sets fire to or burns or causes to be burned or who aids, counsels, or procures the burning of, any structure, forest land, or property.[50]

A structure is defined as "any building, or commercial or public tent, bridge, tunnel, or powerplant.."[51] Property includes "real property or personal property, other than a structure or forest land."[52]

Essentially, there are two elements for the crime of arson. First, the defendant must have set fire to, burned, or caused to be burned any structure, forest land, or property. The property does not have to be completely destroyed for the crime to be complete. Second, the burning must have been done willfully and maliciously. The definition of arson makes it clear that intent is required for the crime. A fire that is of accidental or unintentional origin is not considered to be arson. PC §452 discusses a less serious crime, that of **unlawfully causing a fire**. This crime is defined as,

> A person is guilty of unlawfully causing a fire when he recklessly sets fire to or burns or causes to be burned, any structure, forest land or property.

The key difference between this crime and arson is that unlawfully causing a fire only requires the defendant to have acted recklessly, rather than willfully and maliciously.

In most cases, arson involves the burning of the personal property of another person. However, according to PC §451(d), the burning of one's own personal property may be considered arson if one of the following conditions apply:

1. The fire was set with an intent to defraud (for example, the offender sets fire to an insured building with the intent to collect the insurance money and thereby defraud the insurance company).
2. The property of another person is also injured or destroyed.
3. Another person is injured due to the fire.

The state also recognizes the crime of **aggravated arson**, which is defined in PC §451.5(a). The statute states that,

> Any person who willfully, maliciously, deliberately, with premeditation, and with intent to cause injury to one or more persons or to cause damage to property under circumstances likely to produce injury to one or more persons or to cause damage to one or more structures or inhabited dwellings, sets fire to, burns, or causes to be burned, or aids, counsels, or procures the burning of any residence, structure, forest land, or property is guilty of aggravated arson if one or more of the following aggravating factors exists:
>
> (1) The defendant has been previously convicted of arson on one or more occasions within the past 10 years.
>
> (2) (A) The fire caused property damage and other losses in excess of five million dollars ($5,000,000).
>
> (B) In calculating the total amount of property damage and other losses under subparagraph (A), the court shall consider the cost of fire suppression...
>
> (3) The fire caused damage to, or the destruction of, five or more inhabited structures.

It is often difficult to obtain accurate estimates of the rate of arson because only those fires which have been determined to be the result of willful or malicious burning are included; if the origin of the fire cannot be proved to be willful or malicious, then the fire may not be classified as an arson.

The punishments for arson are set forth in PC §451, as follows:

(a) Arson that causes great bodily injury is a felony punishable by imprisonment in the state prison for five, seven, or nine years.
(b) Arson that causes an inhabited structure or inhabited property to burn is a felony punishable by imprisonment in the state prison for three, five, or eight years.
(c) Arson of a structure or forest land is a felony punishable by imprisonment in the state prison for two, four, or six years.
(d) Arson of property is a felony punishable by imprisonment in the state prison for 16 months, two, or three years.

The punishment for felony arson may be increased by a three- to- five-year enhancement if there are aggravating circumstances, such as are listed in PC §451.1. These include:

- A prior conviction of arson under PC §451 or PC §452
- Emergency personnel (firefighters, peace officers, etc.) suffered great bodily injury as a result of the offense
- Great bodily injury to multiple victims occurred during a single violation of PC §451
- Multiple structures burned during a single violation of PC §451
- The fire was set using a delayed ignition device or a device designed to accelerate the fire

Aggravated arson is punishable by imprisonment in the state prison for a period of ten years to life and will not be eligible for parole release for at least ten years.[53]

Finally, according to PC §452, the punishment for unlawfully causing a fire is:

(a) Unlawfully causing a fire that causes great bodily injury is a felony punishable by imprisonment in the state prison for two, four or six years, or by imprisonment in the county jail for not more than one year, or by a fine, or by both such imprisonment and fine.
(b) Unlawfully causing a fire that causes an inhabited structure or inhabited property to burn is a felony punishable by imprisonment in the state prison for two, three or four years, or by imprisonment in the county jail for not more than one year, or by a fine, or by both such imprisonment and fine.
(c) Unlawfully causing a fire of a structure or forest land is a felony punishable by imprisonment in the state prison for 16 months, two or three years, or by imprisonment in the county jail for not more than six months, or by a fine, or by both such imprisonment and fine.

The penalty for unlawfully causing a fire may be increased by a one- to- three-year enhancement if there are aggravating circumstances similar to those listed in PC 451.[55]

HATE CRIMES

Hate or bias crimes are not specifically included among the UCR's eight index crimes. However, the FBI began to collect data on this category of crime after President George Bush signed the Hate Crimes Statistics Act into law in 1990. The UCR defines hate or bias crimes as "those offenses motivated in part or singularly by personal prejudice against others because of a diversity—race, sexual orientation, religion, ethnicity/national origin, or disability.[55]

The California Office of the Attorney General defines a hate crime as:

> any criminal act or attempted criminal act that is motivated by hatred based on race, ethnicity, national origin, religion, gender, sexual orientation or mental/physical disability.[56]

In 1989, PC §13023 was passed by the State Legislature. This statute requires all local law enforcement agencies in the state to report to the California Department of Justice information on "any criminal acts or attempted criminal acts to cause physical injury, emotional suffering, or property damage where there is a reasonable cause to believe that the crime was motivated, in whole or in part, by the victim's race, ethnicity, religion, gender, sexual orientation, national origin, or physical or mental disability." The California Department of Justice is required to submit an annual report to the State Legislature no later than July 1st, analyzing the results of this information. Every law enforcement agency in the state participates in this reporting program, providing information on the type of crime, the location of the crime, the type of bias motivation, the number of victims, and the number of suspects.[57]

According to the Department of Justice 2001 annual report on hate crime in California,[58] there were a total of 2,261 reported hate crimes in the state during 2001. This is an increase of 15.5 percent over the number of hate crimes reported during 2000. The majority (73 percent) of the hate crimes reported in 2001 were crimes against persons, such as intimidation, simple and aggravated assault, and robbery, while the remaining 27 percent were property crimes such as vandalism, burglary, arson, and larceny theft. The most common violent hate crime was intimidation and the most common property hate crime was vandalism/destruction of property.

In 2001, the most frequent motivation was the race, ethnicity, or national origin of the victim, including over 67 percent of all reported hate crimes in the state. Other motivations included the victim's sexual orientation (19 percent), religion (13 percent), gender (0.7 percent) and physical or mental disability (0.2 percent). The Department of Justice annual report points out that "Hate crime events specifically targeting Arab or Middle Eastern victims ... increased by 345.8 percent over last year's total for this bias motivation category."[59] The report attributes much of this increase to the events of September 11, 2001.

NOTES

1. Recent issues of the *Uniform Crime Reports* may be viewed online on the Federal Bureau of Investigation's website (http://www.fbi.gov/ucr/ucr.htm)
2. PC §190(a)
3. *Ibid*
4. See, e.g., PC §190(b); PC §190(d); PC §190.05
5. PC §192(b)
6. See, e.g., *People v. Clark* (1982) 130 Cal.App.3d 371, 377, 181 Cal.Rptr. 682
7. *People v. Burroughs* (1984) 35 Cal.3d 824, 833, 201 Cal.Rptr. 319, 678 P.wd 894
8. PC§191.5 and PC §192(c)(1-3)
9. PC §192(c)(1)
10. PC §192 (c)(2)
11. PC §192 (c)(3)
12. PC §192 (c)(4)
13. PC §199
14. *Uniform Crime Reports* (http://www.fbi.gov/ucr/ucr.htm)
15. PC §263
16. PC §264.1
17. PC §261.5
18. PC §261.5(b)
19. PC §261.5(d)
20. PC §261.6
21. PC §261.7
22. PC §264.1
23. *People v. Dillon* (1983) 34 Cal.3d 441, 462, 194 Cal.Rptr. 390, 668 P.2d 697
24. *People v. Morales* (1975) 49 Cal. App.3d 134, 139, 122 Cal.Rptr. 157
25. *People v. Hill* (2000) 23 Cal.4th 853, 859-861, 98 Cal.Rptr.2d 254, 3 P.3d 898
26. *Uniform Crime Reports* (http://www.fbi.gov/ucr/ucr.htm)
27. PC §241(a)
28. PC §241(b)
29. PC §241.2(a)(1)
30. PC §241.3(a)
31. PC §241.6
32. PC §243(a)
33. See e.g., PC §243 (b-c)
34. PC §243.4(a)
35. *Ibid*
36. PC §243.4(b)
37. PC §243.4(i)
38. PC §243.4(j)
39. See the original version of PC §459 enacted in 1872
40. *Uniform Crime Reports* (http://www.fbi.gov/ucr/ucr.htm)

41. *People v. Massey* (1961) 196 Cal.App.2d 230, 236, 16 Cal.Rptr, 402
42. *People v. Martinez* (4th Dist.2002) 95 Cal.App.4th 581, 585-586, 115 Cal.Rptr.2d 574
43. PC §461
44. *Uniform Crime Reports* (http://www.fbi.gov/ucr/ucr.htm)
45. PC §484(a)
46. *People v. Moore* (1970) 4 Cal.App.3d 668, 670, 84 Cal.Rptr. 771
47. *People v. Meyer* (1888) 75 Cal. 383, 384-385, 17 P.431
48. *Uniform Crime Reports* (http://www.fbi.gov/ucr/ucr.htm)
49. *Ibid*
50. PC §451
51. PC §450(a)
52. PC §450(c)
53. PC §451.5(b-c)
54. PC §451.1(a)
55. Recent issues of the FBI's *Hate Crime Statistics* may be viewed online on the FBI's website (http://www.fbi.gov/ucr/ucr.htm)
56. *Hate Crime in California 2001*. Available on the web site of Office of the Attorney General (http://caag.state.ca.us/cjsc/publications/hatecrimes/hc01/preface.pdf)
57. *Ibid*
58. *Ibid*
59. *Ibid*, p.iii

CHAPTER 4

THE POLICE IN CALIFORNIA

INTRODUCTION

There are many levels of police agencies in America today, including federal law enforcement, state police, county sheriff's agencies, and city police. In California, any city meeting the standards of the State Legislature may draw up a charter and incorporate. According to the California Constitution, any incorporated city may set up its own city police force.[1] Because of this, there are almost 600 separate law enforcement agencies in California today. Most of these are city departments, each of which has its own chief, its own organization, and its own policies and procedures. In addition, there are 58 county sheriffs' departments, one state police agency (the California Highway Patrol), and a wide variety of special-purpose law enforcement agencies.

In 2001, there were a total of 108,208 persons employed full-time in law enforcement. Of these, 72,119 (67%) were sworn officers and 36,089 (33%) were civilians. The majority of the sworn officers (52%) worked in police departments, 35% worked in sheriff's departments, 10% were employed by the California Highway Patrol, and the remainder (3%) were employed by other law enforcement agencies (e.g., university police, state parks and recreation, rapid transit police, etc.).[2]

LOCAL POLICING

The majority of the police departments in California are local or city departments. In most cases, the police chief is appointed by the head of the city's political system (city manager, mayor, commissioner, etc.) and approved by the city council. Because of this, it is a very political position. If a new city manager is elected, the appointment of a new police chief often follows soon afterwards. Every local department is independent of every other department. The goals, purposes, and priorities vary greatly among departments, with each local agency responding to the needs and desires of the population it serves. All municipal police departments are full-service police agencies which provide a wide range of police services, including law enforcement, order maintenance, and service. Currently, the Los Angeles Police Department, a local city department, is the largest police agency in California.

The Los Angeles Police Department

The discovery of gold at Sutter's Mill and the gold rush that followed led to a sudden increase in immigration into California from around the world. In addition, the end of the Mexican War and California's new status as a state also resulted in the arrival of many new settlers. One result of this was an immediate lack of law and order, a gap that was filled in part by vigilante justice. In 1850, the Los Angeles County Sheriff's Department was formed and two years later, the Los Angeles Rangers were organized. The Rangers was a volunteer unit of 100 men created to assist the county sheriff and the city marshal after the city's second city marshal was murdered. The Rangers were eventually followed by a new agency, the Los Angeles City Guards. However, neither force was very effective.

According to the Los Angeles Police Department's web site[3], the **Los Angeles Police Department** (LAPD) was created in 1869.. It originally consisted of six full-time paid police officers led by the City Marshal. The LAPD's first horse patrol was developed in 1875 and officers assigned to this duty received a higher salary than those who walked a beat on foot. In 1875, the monthly salary of a foot patrolman in the LAPD was $90. Mounted officers received $95 and the city marshal's monthly salary was $105. The horse patrol was disbanded in 1916. The first African-American officers in the LAPD were hired in 1886.

In 1889, John M. Glass became Chief of the LAPD. He originated the first entry-level standards for applicants and developed the beginnings of police professionalism. However, by the early 1900s, political machines had increasingly taken control of the LAPD, significantly affecting its policies. Between 1920 and 1940, Los Angeles was almost totally run by "bosses"who controlled elected officials and dictated police appointments and promotions, leading to serious levels of corruption and vice in the city. The department was controlled in great part by the Mayor's office, which may help to explain the exceptionally high turnover in the office of the Chief of Police during the first quarter of the decade.

The LAPD is also noted for hiring the first female police officer in the United States to be given the power of arrest. Alice Stebbins Wells was appointed hired on September 12, 1910. Her duties included the supervision and enforcement of laws affecting places of public amusement such as picture shows, skating rinks, and dance halls. She also maintained a general information bureau to provide police department-related advice to women. Officer Wells organized the International Policewomen's Association in 1915, persuaded the University of California to offer the first university course specifically focusing on the work of women police officers, helped to create the Women's Peace Officers Association of California and served as its first president, and later served as the LAPD historian until her retirement in 1940.

In 1923, August Vollmer (then Chief of the Berkeley Police Department) agreed to serve as the Chief of the LAPD for one year. Vollmer was a noted reformer and police administrator who made significant changes in the organization of the LAPD, improving the working conditions, establishing new standards of professionalism, and beginning the development of what would later become the LAPD's Scientific Investigation Division. Unfortunately, when his year ended, the political machine again took over and corruption dominated both the LAPD and local city government until the late 1930s, when a new mayor became determined to clean up the government.

There were a number of notable advances within the LAPD during the next few decades. The department's first air patrol was developed in 1931, as was the first use of two-way police radios to allow citizen calls to be broadcast directly to officers in patrol cars. The department boasted a response rate of less than three minutes to any citizen call for service. In 1943, the "Zoot Suit Riots", which began when fights broke out between sailors and Mexican Americans, led to four days of injuries and property damage in the east-central part of Los Angeles.

In 1950, William H. Parker took office as Chief of the LAPD. He served as chief until his death 16 years later; the longest term in the history of the department to date. Parker's contributions to the LAPD included streamlining the department, emphasizing discipline and order, ensuring that the general public was kept aware of department activities, and becoming a pioneer in narcotics enforcement. Chief Parker was the most honored and respected chief in the history of the LAPD; the administrative headquarters of the department was named Parker Center after his death to honor him.

Another well-known Chief of the LAPD was Daryl F. Gates, who took office in 1978, during a period of severe budget and personnel cuts. In 1985, despite the fact that Los Angeles was one of the largest cities in the United States (second only to New York City), the department had only 6,900 sworn officers. The NYPD had almost 29,000 sworn officers and Chicago, which was the third largest city in the U.S. at this time, had over 12,000 officers. In response, the Chief recruited over 55,00 civilian volunteers to aid the department and hired over 1,000 civilians to free sworn officers for field duty. Chief Gates also is notable for his creation of both the Drug Abuse Resistance Education (DARE) program and of Special Weapons and Tactics (SWAT) teams.

The results of the Rodney King trial in 1992 led to the acquittal of four LAPD officers and to rioting around the United States. Chief Gates retired and was replaced by Chief Willie L. Williams, the first African American chief and the first in over 40 years to be hired from outside the department. Chief Williams served for five years.

The LAPD has continued to grow and expand over the years. Today it is the largest police agency in the state of California. In 2000, the department had over 9,000 sworn officers and over 3,000 civilian employees. Of the sworn officers, 81 percent were male and 19 percent female. Approximately 46 percent of the officers were Caucasian, 33 percent were Hispanic, and 14 percent were African American. In the 2000/2001 fiscal year, the department's budget was over $835 million.[4]

Currently, the minimum entrance requirements for the LAPD include:

- minimum age of 21 at date of hire
- high school graduate or the equivalent
- U.S. citizen or a permanent resident alien who is eligible and has applied for U.S. citizenship
- no felony convictions
- no misdemeanor convictions that would prevent the applicant from carrying a gun
- no history of criminal or improper conduct, no poor employment, military, or driving record
- a responsible financial history with no past due or delinquent accounts
- a valid California drivers license
- good physical condition and excellent health
- uncorrected distance vision of no more than 20/40 unless soft contacts are worn
- weight appropriate to height and build

Applicants who meet these requirements must go through a variety of tests, including a written civil service examination, a physical abilities test, a background check, medical, polygraph, and psychological examinations, and an oral interview. Recruits go through a total of 1,064 hours of training (28 weeks), studying a wide variety of subjects including California law and rules of evidence, the laws of arrest, search and seizure, patrol techniques, firearm techniques, defensive techniques, first aid, and LAPD-specific policies and procedures. Academy graduates then go through an 11-month field-training program that continues for the rest of the recruit officer's period of probation.

In 2003, new recruits were hired at a starting salary of $46,771. However, candidates who have a two- or four-year college degree, or who have prior experience as a sworn police officer, will receive a higher starting salary. There are a variety of additional pay and bonus opportunities within the department, including longevity pay and bilingual premiums.[5]

The LAPD is probably one of the most familiar police departments because of its frequent appearance on television and in the movies. Some of the more famous television programs that have either included actual LAPD officers or have had actors portraying them are *Dragnet*, *Adam-12*, *T.J. Hooker*, *COPS*, *LAPD: Life on the Beat*, *Hunter*, and *America's Most Wanted.* Movies about the LAPD include *The Onion Field*, *The New Centurions*, *The Blue Knight*, *LA Confidential*, *Lethal Weapon*, *Terminator*, *To Live or Die in L.A.*, and *Die Hard.*

COUNTY POLICING

Each of the 58 counties in California has a separate sheriff's department. According to the California State Constitution, all county sheriffs are elected, rather than appointed.[6] As a result, partisan politics significantly influences county police agencies in the state. The Constitution does not set forth any legal minimum requirements which must be met by candidates running for sheriff; for example, candidates for sheriff are not required to have attended a police academy or to have any practical policing experience of any kind.

Sheriffs' departments in California are full service police agencies that provide police services to all unincorporated areas of the county. In addition, incorporated cities that do not wish to set up their own city police department may contract out to their county sheriff's department for police services. Section 26600-26616 of the California Government Code (GC) outlines the duties of sheriffs and deputy sheriffs in California. Sheriff's departments in California are not only responsible for providing law enforcement services to the county but also for running the county jail, maintaining security in all county courts, serving civil and criminal processes, and providing assistance when needed to local departments within the county. This assistance can range from operating a county-wide crime lab to assisting a local department with a criminal investigation.

The Los Angeles County Sheriff's Department

The **Los Angeles County Sheriff's Department** (LASD) is the largest sheriff's department in the world. Like the LAPD, the creation of the LASD was influenced by the gold rush and the resulting immigration into California. During the gold rush period, over 100,000 people rushed to the gold fields of California, living under extremely chaotic and lawless conditions that led to vigilante justice and a form of "lynch law." Arrivals included not only honest gold prospectors but escaped criminals, outlaws, and a wide variety of troublemakers.

In 1850, the Sheriff's Department of Los Angeles was founded with one elected sheriff and two deputies. They were responsible for enforcing law and order in the vast area known as Los Angeles County, which at that time also included the present counties of Kern, Orange, San Bernardino, and Ventura. The sheriff was elected annually until 1882, at which time the term was increased to a period of two years. The term was increased to its present length of four years in 1894.

Two years after the Sheriff's Department was created, the Los Angeles Rangers were organized as a volunteer posse of 100 men whose purpose was to assist the sheriff and the city marshal. The early job of sheriff in Los Angeles County was not a healthy one: in 1857, the county sheriff and several members of his posse were killed. The following year another sheriff was murdered during an arrest attempt.

The first woman sheriff's deputy in the United States was appointed by the LASD in 1912. The civil service merit system was installed one year later, eliminating the fee system that had been in use until that time. This significantly reduced opportunities for corruption and helped to modernize the department. LASD deputies wore civilian clothes until a formal uniform was adopted in 1928. They did not drive marked patrol cars until 1932.[7]

In 2002, the LASD was the primary law enforcement agency for unincorporated Los Angeles County as well as for 41 incorporated cities that contract with the department for their law enforcement services. The department has 8,915 sworn officers and almost 6,000 professional staff. Of the sworn officers, approximately 85 percent are male and 15 percent female. Approximately, 55 percent are white, 29 percent Hispanic, 10 percent black, and 4 percent Asian. During 2002, the LASD handled almost 89,000 incidents, and made over 95,000 arrests.[8]

The LASD is divided into ten separate divisions. These include three patrol divisions, Detective Division, Custody Operations Division, Correctional Services Division, Court Services Division, Technical Services Division, Office of Administrative Services, and Personnel and Training Division. The **Detective Division** of the LASD investigates crimes in unincorporated Los Angeles County. In addition, they may be asked to assist local agencies within the county on specific cases. The **Court Services Division** is responsible for maintaining security in all superior and municipal courts in LA County. The division provides court bailiffs, detains and transports prisoners to and from the courts, serves and enforces all civil and criminal processes, and provides judicial protection. The **Custody Operations Division** is responsible for the operation of the county's eight jail facilities, while the **Correctional Services Division** includes various supplementary units and special program centers that provide support for the jails. The **Technical Services Division** is responsible for providing support to the LASD, including communications, management of all departmental vehicles, the implementation and management of data and information systems, records and identification, and the operation of one of the largest full-service scientific crime laboratories in the U.S.[9]

In October 2002, the LASD created a new **Office of Homeland Security**, in response to the events of September 11, 2001. The Office is responsible for coordinating and commanding all units and bureaus within the LASD that have a link to local homeland security.

The San Francisco County Sheriff's Department

San Francisco is the only county in California with common county and city boundaries. Therefore, the law enforcement duties are divided between the San Francisco County Sheriff's Department and the San Francisco Police Department. The city police are responsible for routine street patrol and make most arrests in the jurisdiction. **The San Francisco Sheriff's Department's** (SFSD) has a wide variety of responsibilities that include law enforcement, crime prevention, and corrections. Currently, the SFSD has approximately 850 sworn deputies and 100 civilian employees.[10]

The SFSD's **Custody Division** is responsible for running the county jail system, which includes five jails, a jail ward in San Francisco General Hospital, and an intake and release facility. The jail system houses an average daily population of 2,200 prisoners. Approximately 55,000 individuals are booked into the county jails every year. The Division is also responsible for transferring arrested individuals from police stations to the intake jail and for transporting prisoners between jail facilities and the courts. The SFSD also operates a number of jail alternative programs, including:

- a home detention program that uses electronic and video monitoring to confirm curfew compliance

- the Sheriff's Work Alternative Program (SWAP) and Post Release Educational Program (PREP) in which offenders are assigned to a combination of PREP classes and SWAP work crews and must participate at least two days a week

- various residential county parole facilities which include licensed residential substance abuse programs in which offenders participate upon referral by the court or after in-jail participation in a similar program

The SFSD's **Civil Division** carries out civil court judgments of various types, including serving various court papers such as civil bench warrants and subpoenas, performing evictions, and collecting fees in advance for services performed by the SFSD. The department also provides security for all city and county criminal and civil courts. The department's responsibilities in this area include providing court bailiffs, escorting defendants to court, maintaining security in the court buildings, transporting psychiatric patients to and from medical facilities, and responding to emergency calls from the courts.

The **Courts Division** provides security for all criminal and civil courts in the county. Deputies assigned to this division serve as court bailiffs, provide security for court buildings, transport defendants to and from court, and respond to any emergency calls from the courts.

STATE POLICING

There are two main types of **state police agencies** within the United States. Some states, such as Pennsylvania, operate a **centralized** full-service state police agency which includes both highway patrol functions and criminal investigation. However, other states, including California, separate or **decentralize** the two functions, keeping criminal investigations separate from the uniformed highway patrol. In California, the **State Attorney General** is responsible for criminal investigation and law enforcement within the state. Meanwhile, uniformed officers of the **California Highway Patrol** focus specifically on patrolling the state highways.

The California Attorney General

The office of the **California Attorney General** was created in 1850 to serve as the head of law enforcement within the state of California. According to the California Constitution,

> ...the Attorney General shall be the chief law officer of the State. It shall be the duty of the Attorney General to see that the laws of the State are uniformly and adequately enforced.[11]

The Attorney General is elected to a four-year term by the voters in a statewide election and is limited to a total of two terms. The Attorney General supervises all county sheriffs and district attorneys.[12]

The **California Department of Justice** (DOJ) provides the Attorney General with the support needed to fulfil these various constitutional obligations. Through the DOJ, the Attorney General assists law enforcement agencies within the state when necessary, coordinates state-wide narcotics enforcement efforts, provides crime lab, forensic science, and identification and information services to county and local agencies, and participates in criminal investigations.[13]

Possibly one of the most well-known resources operated by the DOJ falls under "**Megan's Law**," which provides the public with information on registered sex offenders. The law is named after a seven-year-old New Jersey girl, Megan Kanka, who was raped and killed by a known child molester who, unknown to the Kankas, had moved into a home across the street from them. This legislation, which was sponsored by the Attorney General and signed into law in 1996, increases public safety by providing the public with specific information on the location of dangerous sex offenders and by allowing local police to inform the public about serious sex offenders who live in, work in, or frequent their community. The DOJ maintains the Megan's Law Web Application, a computerized database of registered sex offenders which can be accessed by members of the public.

The DOJ also runs a variety of other law enforcement-related services. For example, the **Criminal Justice Statistics Center** collects, examines, analyzes, and produces reports on data on crime and the criminal justice system in California. The Attorney General's **Crime and Violence Prevention Center** provides information, resources, and technical assistance in areas such as community policing, domestic violence, elder abuse, hate crimes, school safety, drug and alcohol abuse, child abuse, and high tech crimes. The **Child Protection Program** focuses specifically on child physical, sexual, and emotional abuse, and on child neglect. The **Bureau of Forensic Sciences** runs a number of full-service crime laboratories located throughout the state as well as providing criminalistic support at crime scenes to local law enforcement agencies. The **Investigative Support Crime Analysis Unit** assists local law enforcement agencies in identifying and apprehending violent serious offenders by coordinating information on unsolved crimes. The unit focuses primarily on serious violent crimes such as murder, kidnapping, robbery, rape, and sexual assault.

One of the DOJ's newest initiatives is the **California Anti-Terrorism Information Center**, which was created in partnership with law enforcement agencies throughout the state, and in the federal government, after the events of September 11th. The purpose of this program is to provide statewide intelligence support to local law enforcement agencies in the war on terrorism.

The California Highway Patrol

The **California Highway Patrol** (CHP) was created on August 4, 1929 by an act of the California State Legislature. The law gave the CHP the authority to enforce traffic laws on all county and state highways in California. By 1939, the CHP had a total of 730 uniformed officers. The Patrol's responsibilities were reorganized after World War II and, in 1947, the Department of the California Highway Patrol was established.

The responsibilities of the Patrol have increased significantly as the CHP has expanded. Today, the primary mission of the CHP is "to ensure safety and provide service to the public as they utilize the highway transportation system and to assist local government during emergencies when requested."[14]

The "Newhall Incident" is considered by the CHP to be the most tragic event in the department's history. The event occurred on April 6, 1970, when four CHP officers were killed in a 4 1/2 minute gun battle. The first two officers were responding to a radio call concerning a vehicle carrying someone who had displayed a weapon on a highway. After spotting the car, they called for backup and stopped the car in the parking lot of a restaurant. As the officers approached the car, the passenger door opened and the passenger suspect shot one of the officers. The vehicle's driver then shot the other officer. Both officers died instantly of their wounds.

The backup officers arrived shortly after and were immediately fired upon by the two suspects. Both officers died of wounds received and one of the suspects was also wounded during the exchange of gunfire. The two suspects escaped in their vehicle but later abandoned the car and split up. One suspect broke into a house and held a man in the house as hostage. CHP officers shot tear gas into the house before entering it but the suspect killed himself with a shotgun he had stolen from the first officer killed. The other suspect was later captured, stood trial, and was convicted of four counts of first-degree murder. He originally received a sentence of death but in 1972 the California Supreme Court declared the death penalty to be cruel and unusual punishment. In 1973, the suspect's punishment was changed to life in prison. He spent some time in Folsom State Prison and was later moved to Pelican Bay State Prison.

The result of this incident was to focus attention on police officer safety. After the Newhall Incident, the CHP completely revised the procedures to be followed during high-risk and felony stops, increasing the emphasis on officer safety at every step of the procedures. More than thirty years after the event, officer safety and more comprehensive training are still a primary concern among the CHP.

In the late 1970s and early 1980s, the CHP became nationally known through the television show *CHiPs*. A reunion movie, *CHiPs 99*, aired in October 1998.

In 1994, then-Governor of California, Pete Wilson, proposed that the CHP and the California State Police (CSP) be consolidated into one statewide law enforcement agency. At the time, the CSP was primarily responsible for the protection of state property, facilities, employees, and officials. Governor Wilson's goal was to incorporate the CSP into the CHP, creating an agency that would provide law enforcement service for the public, state employees, and state facilities. An analysis of the proposal suggested that merging the two departments would result in an increased level of public safety and service, but not produce higher costs. The merger was officially completed on July 12, 1995. At that time, the 271 uniformed CSP officers became CHP sworn officers and most non-uniformed CSP employees were also merged into the CHP.

The merger greatly broadened the responsibilities of the CHP. The CHP is now responsible for providing patrol services for the Department of Motor Vehicles (DMV), the Employment Development Department (EDD), and the Department of Transportation. They provide security services at hearings of the DMV, the EDD, the California Courts of Appeals, and the Department of Consumer Affairs. The CHP also serves tax seizure and arrest warrants for the Board of Equalization and the Franchise Tax Board. The CHP patrol the State Capital and Legislative Office Building and are also responsible for protecting the Governor, other constitutional officers and dignitaries, anyone who works in or visits a state building, and all state property.

The CHP is also highly involved in educating the public concerning driver safety issues. They have developed public awareness programs promoting such things as the use of safety belts, the use of Designated Drivers when drinking, the use of child safety seats, and the use of motorcycle and bicycle helmets.

In 2000, the CHP had over 6,500 sworn officers and over 3,200 civilian employees. In addition to providing services to motorists on state and interstate highways, the CHP employs a limited number of investigators who focus specifically on vehicle thefts. Other criminal investigations are the responsibility of other state agencies, particularly the Attorney General's Office and the Department of Justice.

Other State Law Enforcement Agencies

There are a number of other state agencies which employ investigators and whose responsibilities include criminal investigation. Some of these include:

- **California Department of Alcoholic Beverage Control** – responsible for regulating the manufacture and sale of alcoholic beverages and for investigating violations of the state's Alcoholic Beverage Control Act (e.g., underage drinking)

- **California Department of Consumer Affairs** – responsible for protecting consumers from fraudulent, deceptive, or unlawful business practices

- **California State Fire Marshal** – responsible for fire prevention in the state, including arson investigation

- **California Department of Fish and Game** – responsible for enforcing the wildlife laws within the state, including those relating to fishing and hunting

- **California Department of Insurance** – responsible for overseeing the insurance industry, regulating, investigating, and auditing insurance businesses, protecting the public, and enforcing the laws of the California Insurance Code

- **California Department of Motor Vehicles** – responsible for enforcing laws relating to the ownership and registration of motor vehicles and for the licensing and regulation of driving schools, traffic violator schools, vehicle manufacturers, transporters, dealers, distributors, and salespersons

- **California State Park and Recreation Commission** – responsible for enforcing laws and regulations which relate to the California system of state parks and recreational facilities and for ensuring the safety of visitors and personnel

POLICE TRAINING

Police departments today require highly qualified and well-trained officers. In 1959, the **California Commission on Peace Officers Standards and Training** (POST) was created to develop minimum professional standards for selection and training of law enforcement officers throughout the state.

The Commission consists of fourteen members who are appointed by the governor with the advice and consent of the Senate. The Attorney General also serves as an *ex officio* member of the commission. The Commission includes sworn officers, members of the public, and criminal justice educators and trainers. Commission members serve terms of three years. There is no compensation for service on the Commission.[15]

The Commission focuses on three primary areas which are believed to be important to effective law enforcement in California. These include:

- Developing and regularly updating job-related selection standards to ensure state-wide consistency in selection standards of peace officers in California

- Making certain that all law enforcement officers in California have access to training that will allow them to obtain the skills, knowledge, attitudes, and behaviors consistent with the job requirements and expectations

- Providing leadership development programs and management counseling services to facilitate positive and productive organizational environments[16]

Participation in the POST program is voluntary, rather than mandatory. Agencies which participate in POST agree to abide by POST selection and training standards and may be eligible for financial assistance to train personnel. Currently, all California county sheriffs' departments, all city police departments, and all University of California and California State University system campuses participate in POST. In addition, all state agencies, a number of district attorneys' offices, and a variety of other departments which employ peace officers participate in the program. In total, over 400 law enforcement agencies in California participate in the POST program.[17]

Participating agencies agree to subscribe to a set of minimum selection and training standards established by POST as a way of standardizing law enforcement employment requirements throughout the state. Currently, the minimum selection standards for peace officers employed by agencies participating in the POST program include the following:

- Be at least 18 years old
- Be a U.S. citizen or permanent resident alien who is eligible for and has applied for U.S. citizenship
- Be fingerprinted for a search of local, state, and national fingerprint files to reveal any criminal record
- Be of good moral character (to be determined by a thorough background investigation)
- Be a high school graduate, have passed the GED, or have a two- or four-year degree from an accredited college or university
- Have no felony convictions
- Be medically and psychologically suitable (as determined by medical and psychological examinations)
- Be a high school graduate or pass the GED
- Be personally interviewed by the agency head or a representative prior to employment
- Be able to read and write at the level needed to perform the job of peace officer and pass a POST test of reading and writing ability.[18]

Departments participating in POST may require applicants to meet selection standards that are higher than those set by POST, and to undergo additional testing procedures. For example, a local department may have vision and hearing requirements, even though there are no minimum standards set by POST. Additional selection procedures may include a drug screening examination, a polygraph examination, and a physical ability test (such as an obstacle course).

The Commission also regulates minimum training standards and requires peace officers to complete a basic academy training course of at least 664 hours. There are 39 certified basic training academies, most of which run programs of 17 to 20 weeks in length (although some may be longer). In addition, the Commission requires recruits who have graduated from the basic course to go through a Field Training Program lasting at least ten weeks.

NOTES

1. California State Constitution, Article 11, Section 5b
2. Information obtained from the *California Criminal Justice Profile, 2001*, available on the home page of the California Office of the Attorney General (http://justice.hdcdojnet.state.ca.us/cjsc_stats/prof01/index.htm)
3. Los Angeles Police Department web site (http://www.lapdonline.org/)
4. Information obtained from the *Los Angeles Police Department Annual Report, 2000*, which is available on LAPD web site
5. Los Angeles Police Department web site
6. California State Constitution, Article 11, Section 4c
7. Los Angeles Sheriff's Department web site (http://www.lasd.org/)
8. Information obtained from the *Year in Review, 2002*, which is available on the LASD web site
9. Los Angeles Sheriff's Department web site
10. San Francisco Sheriff's Department web site (http://www.ci.sf.ca.us/sheriff/home.htm)
11. California State Constitution, Article 5, Section 13
12. *Ibid*
13. California Department of Justice, Office of the Attorney General web site (http://caag.state.ca.us/)
14. California Highway Patrol web site (http://www.chp.ca.gov/index.html)
15. PC 13500
16. State of California Commission on Peace Officer Standards and Training, *Strategic Plan 2002: Making a Bold Adjustment*. Available on the POST web site (http://www.post.ca.gov/about/plan.asp#exec)
17. *Ibid*
18. POST web site

CHAPTER 5

THE COURT SYSTEM IN CALIFORNIA

INTRODUCTION

The criminal court system in California is a two-tiered system that strongly resembles the federal system. It consists of a state Supreme Court, a number of District (or intermediate) Courts of Appeal, and superior (trial) courts. California's judicial branch is the largest court system in the world.

UNITED STATES FEDERAL COURTS

Although they are not specifically part of the California State Court system, there are four **U.S. District Courts** that sit in California.[1] These are the trial courts of the federal system. The Northern District sits at San Francisco, San Jose, Oakland, and Eureka. The Eastern District Court sits in Sacramento, Fresno, and Redding. The Central District Court sits at Los Angeles, Santa Ana, and San Bernardino. The Southern District Court sits at San Diego.

The **U.S. Courts of Appeals** are the intermediate appellate courts of the federal court system and have appellate jurisdiction only over federal laws. Judges in these courts are nominated by the President of the United States and confirmed by the Senate. California is part of the Ninth Circuit.[2]

THE CALIFORNIA SUPREME COURT

The **California Supreme Court** is the highest court in the state and is the court of last resort in California. Its decisions are binding upon all other courts in the state. The court was established in 1849 in Article VI of the first California State Constitution. Originally, the court consisted of a Chief Justice and two associate justices who were elected and who served six-year terms.[3] Two additional justices were added in 1862 and the term of office was increased to ten years. In 1878 and 1879, the state held a Constitutional Convention to revise the California State Constitution. There were a number of changes made to the judicial system, including the supreme court. The number of justices was increased to the present total of seven, and the term of office increased to the current length of twelve years.

Today, all California Supreme Court justices are appointed by the state governor and confirmed by the Commission on Judicial Appointments. They are then confirmed by the voters at the next upcoming state-wide election. Justices who have completed their term of office must appear on the ballot again for retention if they wish to continue to serve on the court. To be eligible to serve as a justice on the California Supreme Court, an individual must be an attorney admitted to the

California bar or must have served as a judge in a court of record in California for at least ten years immediately preceding the appointment to the Supreme Court.[4]

When the Supreme Court was originally established, it was given appellate jurisdiction in all cases in which the amount in controversy was greater than $200, all cases in which the legality of a tax, toll, impost, or municipal fine was at issue, and all felony matters raising questions of law. The court also had the power to issue writs of *habeas corpus* and all writs necessary to exercise its appellate jurisdiction. Subsequent constitutional amendments have significantly increased the jurisdiction and duties of the court.

Today, the California State Constitution gives the California Supreme Court original jurisdiction in proceedings for extraordinary relief such as *mandamus*, *certiorari*, prohibition, and *habeas corpus*.[5] The first three are various forms of petitions or writs which are used to get a case before court. A writ of *habeas corpus* is a legal procedure which requires a court to review the legality of an individual's detention or imprisonment. The Court also has appellate jurisdiction to review decisions made by the state Courts of Appeal.[6] This allows the Court to decide important legal questions and to maintain uniformity in the state law. The Court may select specific issues in a case to review or it may decide all the issues in a case. In addition, the Court has appellate jurisdiction in all cases in which a sentence of death has been handed down by the trial court.[7] Under California state law, all cases resulting in a capital sentence are automatically appealed directly from the trial court to the Supreme Court of the state.[8] Capital cases are the only ones in which review by the Supreme Court is guaranteed as a right. The Court has the discretion to decide whether or not it will review any non-capital cases. The Court is also responsible for reviewing the recommendations of the Commission on Judicial Performance and the State Bar of California with regards to the discipline of attorneys and judges for misconduct. Appeals from decisions of the California Public Utilities Commission also come directly to the Supreme Court.

As stated above, all capital cases are reviewed by the Supreme Court. However, for a non-capital case to be heard by the Court, a **petition for review** must first be filed with the Court, asking the Court to review the decision made by a lower court in the state. An average of 250 petitions and other matters are considered each week at the regular court conference and at least four justices must agree for a case to be reviewed. Approximately three percent of the petitions for review considered by the Court are granted.[9]

If the petition is granted, the case is assigned to one of the associate justices who prepares a **calendar memorandum** setting forth the facts of the case, analyzing the legal issues involved in the case, and making a recommendation concerning the disposition of the case. Each justice reviews the memorandum and makes suggestions concerning revision. A majority of the justices must agree with the calendar memorandum, or a revised or new version, before the case may move to the next stage of processing.

The actual formal review of the case is known as an **oral argument**. These are held regularly one week a month (with the exceptions of July and August, when no sessions are held). The oral argument phase gives the justices a chance to question the attorneys or the litigants in person about issues raised in legal briefs. In most cases, each side is given no more than 30 minutes to argue its case before the Court. However, in capital cases, the Court may extend the time limit to 45 minutes for each side.

When the oral argument is complete, the justices discuss the case and take a tentative vote. The Court requires the agreement of at least four justices for a decision to be handed down. If the majority vote agrees with the recommendations set forth in the calendar memorandum, the justice who wrote the memorandum is assigned to draft the **majority opinion**, although other justices may write concurring or dissenting opinions. If the majority vote disagrees with the view proposed by the calendar memorandum, the Chief Justice will reassign the case to one of the majority for the preparation of the majority opinion. The majority opinion is circulated to all justices, giving them the opportunity to make changes, revisions, or amendments. The final written opinion will be filed within 90 days after the oral argument is completed.

Finally, the decision will be made available to the public, or **filed**, with the Clerk's Office. The decision does not become final until 30 days after the date of filing, giving both sides time to petition for a rehearing and giving the court time to consider such petitions.[10]

CALIFORNIA DISTRICT COURTS OF APPEAL

California district courts of appeal are California's intermediate appellate courts of review. They were established in 1904 by an amendment to Article 6 of the California Constitution. The original purpose of the amendment was to create a solution to a continuing problem of congestion and delay within the State Supreme Court. The district courts were created to act as a "buffer" between the lower trial courts and the State Supreme Court. By handling the majority of the appellate work in the state, district courts of appeal allow the Supreme Court to review only those cases that raise important legal questions and to ensure that decisions made throughout the state are uniform.

The amendment originally created three appellate districts, each containing a court of appeal with at least one division. A 1966 modification of the Constitution later created an additional three districts. Article VI , Section 3 of the California State Constitution gives the state legislature the constitutional authority to create new districts and divisions. Currently there are six appellate districts in the state. These districts have a total of 19 divisions and over 100 justices.[11] Each district is headquartered in a different city. The First District is headquartered in San Francisco and has 20 justices. The Second is headquartered in Los Angeles and has 32 justices. The Third District is headquartered in Sacramento and has 11 justices. The Fourth District has headquarters in San Diego (9 justices), Riverside (6 justices), and Santa Ana (6 justices). The Fifth District, which is headquartered in Fresno, is unusual in that it is not divided into districts. This district has 10 justices. Finally, the Sixth District is headquartered in San Jose and has 6 justices.

Each district, except the Fifth, is divided into divisions, each of which has a presiding justice and two or more associate justices. These are appointed by the state governor and confirmed by the Commission on Judicial Appointments and must be retained by the public at the next general election and again at the end of each twelve-year term.[12] Eligibility requirements for district court justices are the same as the requirements for justices of the Supreme Court.[13]

According to the California State Constitution,[14] district courts, like the California Supreme Court, have original jurisdiction in *habeas corpus*, *mandamus*, *certiorari*, and prohibition proceedings. The courts have appellate jurisdiction in all cases where the state superior courts have original jurisdiction, except for capital cases, in which the State Supreme Court exercises original mandatory jurisdiction. In addition, the district court has the ability to transfer appeals that are pending in appellate departments of the superior court to itself if the court feels it is necessary to settle important questions of law or to ensure that decisions will be uniform. Each case is decided by a randomly-selected panel of three judges.

The courts of appeal base their decisions on the merits of the case, using the record on appeal; they do not hear additional testimony or retry the case. Unlike the State Supreme Court, the courts of appeal do not hear oral arguments. Their primary purpose is to review the judgement made by the trial court to determine if a legal error was made. The decisions of the courts of appeal may be reviewed by the California Supreme Court, if the Supreme Court feels the case raises an important legal question or that legal issues have been decided inconsistently or non-uniformly in different district courts of appeal.

TRIAL COURTS IN CALIFORNIA

Until 1994, California had three types of trial courts: **Superior Courts**, **Municipal Courts**, and **Justice Courts**. However, a series of constitutional amendments passed between 1995 and 1998 significantly changed the structure of the California trial courts.

Proposition 191 was implemented on January 1, 1995. This constitutional amendment converted all justice courts to municipal courts, so that the state trial court system included only superior and municipal courts. Each court had its own jurisdiction and a specific number of judges, as determined by the State Legislature. The 209 municipal courts had jurisdiction over all criminal misdemeanors and infractions as well as some small claims cases and civil lawsuits. In some situations, felony arraignments and preliminary hearings were also held in the municipal court. The 58 superior courts, one located in each county in the state, had jurisdiction over all felony cases and over all civil cases not under the jurisdiction of the municipal court.

On June 2, 1998, Proposition 220 passed in a statewide primary election by a 64 percent majority. This constitutional amendment permits each county to merge their superior and municipal courts into a single unified superior court. **Court unification** was done on a county-by-county basis and had to be approved by a majority of superior and municipal court judges within each county. The primary goals of court unification were to:

- improve public service by consolidation of court resources
- increase the flexibility of case assignments
- save the taxpayers money

As of February, 2001, all 58 counties had voted to unify their trial courts. Municipal courts have been abolished and all municipal court functions assumed by the new unified superior courts, which now have original trial jurisdiction over all criminal and civil cases. Arraignments preliminary hearings are no longer held in the Municipal Court before the case goes to the superior court. Superior court judges serve terms of six years and are elected by the voters in a county-wide general election. To be eligible to serve as a superior court judge, candidates must be an attorney admitted to practice law in California or must have served as a judge in a court of record in California for at least ten years immediately preceding the election or appointment.[15]

COURT ADMINISTRATION

The Judicial Council of California

The **Judicial Council of California**, which is chaired by the Chief Justice of the California Supreme Court, has been given the responsibility for overseeing and improving the administration of justice in the state. The Council was established in 1926 and is responsible for making recommendations and providing guidelines to all state courts, making annual recommendations to the state legislature and the governor, and adopting and revising the California Rules of Court.[16]

The composition of the Judicial Council is outlined in the California State Constitution and includes:

> the Chief Justice and one other judge of the Supreme Court, 3 judges of courts of appeal, 5 judges of superior courts, 5 judges of municipal courts, 2 nonvoting court administrators, and such other nonvoting members as determined by the voting membership of the council, each appointed by the Chief Justice for a 3-year term pursuant to procedures established by the council; 4 members of the State Bar appointed by its governing body for 3-year terms; and one member of each house of the Legislature appointed as provided by the house.[17]

According to the website of the California Courts,[18] the Judicial Council recently has been involved in a wide variety of activities to bring about improvements to the entire state court system. Some of these activities include:

- Shifting the responsibility for funding trial courts from individual counties to the state, thereby providing a more stable, long-term funding solution for the trial courts
- Advancing the unification of trial courts by advocating the passage of Proposition 220
- Developing a special Task Force on Community Outreach to increase public trust in the state judiciary, educate the public about the court system, and encourage cooperation and collaboration between the state judiciary and communities throughout the state
- Reforming the jury system, including drafting new civil and criminal jury instructions that accurately state the law and that are more easily understandable to jurors, increasing the daily juror reimbursement, and creating a web page for California jurors

- Developing programs to increase access and fairness for minorities and persons with disabilities in the state courts

- Developing a court interpreter program to increase the number and quality of interpreters provided in civil and criminal court proceedings to witnesses and defendants who do not speak and/or understand English. According to Article 1, Section 14 of the California State Constitution, "A person unable to understand English who is charged with a crime has a right to an interpreter throughout the proceedings." Thus, this program is essential for providing defendants with their constitutional right to an interpreter. To become a certified court interpreter, an individual must pass a statewide certification examination, register with the Judicial Council, pay an annual fee (currently $85 per year), attend a Judicial Council Code of Ethics Workshop, and provide proof of ongoing continuing education and professional experience. Some trial courts have permanent positions for interpreters while others hire them by the day as needed.

The Commission on Judicial Appointments

According to the State Constitution, the governor may make appointments to the California Supreme Court and to the various district courts of appeal. However, a 1934 amendment to the Constitution states that these appointments must be confirmed by the Sate Commission on Judicial Appointments. The composition of the Commission is outlined in the Sate Constitution[19] and includes three members: the Chief Justice of the Supreme Court, the State Attorney General, and the senior presiding judge of the district under consideration. If the appointment to be confirmed is for a Supreme Court justice, the third member of the commission is the senior presiding justice of the district courts of appeal.

The Commission, which is based in San Francisco, does not sit regularly but convenes only after the governor nominates or appoints an individual to fill a vacancy on the Supreme Court or a district court of appeal. Public hearings are held by the Commission to review the qualifications of the appointee and the Commission has the power to either confirm or veto the governor's appointment. Article 6, Section 16 of the California State Constitution states that no nomination or appointment made by the governor is final until it has been confirmed by the Commission.

The Commission on Judicial Performance

The California State Constitution[20] also provides for a statewide Commission on Judicial Performance to monitor the behavior of judges in the state and to conduct proceedings against any judge in the state after conducing an investigation. According to the Commission website[21], its mandate is:

> The commission is responsible for the investigation of complaints of judicial misconduct and incapacity and for the discipline of judges, former judges and court commissioners and referees. The commission's authority is limited to investigation and discipline of judicial misconduct, which usually involves conduct in conflict with the Code of Judicial Ethics.

The Commission investigates cases of willful misconduct in office, continual inability or failure to perform the duties of office, conduct on the part of a judge that is prejudicial to the administration of justice in the state and that may be detrimental to the judicial office itself, chronic or habitual intemperance, or a permanent disability that seriously interferes with the performance of the duties of office.[22]

The Commission was established in 1960 and began work in 1961. It was the first permanent agency set up in any state to investigate and deal with judicial misconduct. Today every state has a similar agency, many of which have been modeled after California's plan. In 1994, California voters passed Proposition 190, which significantly increased the power of the Commission. For example, this Proposition gave the Commission the authority to discipline and/or remove California Supreme Court justices and provided for public disciplinary proceedings against judges and former judges. The Proposition also required the Supreme Court to develop and issue a State Code of Judicial Ethics.

Prior to the passage of Proposition 190, the Commission was composed of nine members. However, the Proposition increased the membership to eleven, including:

> one judge of a court of appeal, one judge of a superior court, and one judge of a municipal court, each appointed by the Supreme Court; 2 members of the State Bar of California who have practiced law in this State for 10 years, each appointed by the Governor; and 6 citizens who are not judges, retired judges, or members of the State Bar of California, 2 of whom shall be appointed by the Governor, 2 by the Senate Committee on Rules, and 2 by the Speaker of the Assembly.[23]

State Bar of California

According to Article 6, Section 9 of the California State Constitution,

> the State Bar of California is a public corporation. Every person admitted and licensed to practice law in this State is and shall be a member of the State Bar except while holding office as a judge of a court of record.

Thus, California has an integrated or unified bar, and all licensed attorneys must be members. The Bar is discussed in detail in Sections 6000-6009.3 of the California Business and Professional Code, also known as the State Bar Act. In January 2003, the State Bar had over 191,000 members, making it the largest state bar in the United States.[24] This number includes approximately 40,000 inactive members, who do not currently practice law in the state, and almost 2,000 judges.

Individuals who wish to practice law in California must meet a variety of eligibility requirements and pass a three-day examination set by the State Bar before being certified by the Bar to the State Supreme Court. Eligibility requirements include:

- be at least 18 y ears of age
- be of good moral character

- complete the minimum general and legal education requirements set forth by the State Bar
- pass the California Bar Examination and any other examinations set forth by the State Bar
- be in compliance with any California court-ordered child support or family support obligations

All members must complete at least 25 hours of continuing legal education every three years. This requirement includes at least one hour of education on eliminating bias in the legal system and one hour of education on alcohol abuse and chemical dependency.[25]

The State Bar develops and enforces rules of professional conduct which are binding on all lawyers in California. The Bar also investigates all allegations of attorney misconduct. Charges are heard by the independent State Bar Court, which may issue private or public sanctions, and may recommend to the State Supreme Court that an attorney be suspended or disbarred. These more severe penalties are generally reserved for attorneys who have been involved in professional misconduct or who have been convicted of a serious crime. Members of the State Bar Court are appointed by the State Supreme Court.

CALIFORNIA CRIMINAL COURT PROCEDURES

The basic procedures involved in a criminal trial, including the pretrial activities, are similar in most states. In California, the process begins when the police are notified (or in some other way discover) that a crime has been committed and they initiate an investigation into that crime. The procedures discussed in this section specifically apply to felony offenses; however, the procedures for misdemeanors are extremely similar.

Arrest and Booking

After the police have determined both that a crime has in fact been committed and that a specific person committed the crime, they may place that individual under **arrest**. In California an arrest is defined as "taking a person into custody, in a case and in the manner authorized by law."[26] In some situations, the police may have obtained an **arrest warrant** from a judge. The contents of an arrest warrant are specified in PC §815; any warrant that does not include all the information outlined in this statute is invalid. However, in California, the vast majority of arrests are made by police officers acting without a warrant. PC §836(a) outlines the various situations in which it is lawful to make an arrest without a warrant.

After a suspect has been arrested and taken to the county jail, he/she undergoes the **booking** procedure, which involves entering into the police record various facts about the suspect. At this time, the suspect will be photographed and fingerprinted and may be placed in a police lineup.

Arraignment

After a defendant is taken into custody by the police, he/she has the right to an **arraignment**, or **first appearance**, before a superior court judge. In general, the defendant must be taken before the judge within 48 hours of being arrested, not including Sundays and holidays.[27] At the arraignment, the judge will inform the defendant of his or her constitutional rights and explain the charges that have been brought against the defendant. If the defendant has been charged with a felony or a misdemeanor and cannot afford to hire an attorney, the court at this time will appoint one from the public defender's office. Public defenders are not appointed in cases where the defendant is charged with an infraction because conviction of an infraction in California does not result in a term of incarceration in a jail or prison.

The judge will also decide at this time whether the defendant is entitled to any form of **pretrial release**, including **bail**. Although the U.S. Supreme Court stated in *Stack v. Boyle*[28] that the U.S. Constitution does not guarantee the right to bail, the California State Constitution does provide a substantive right to bail in many cases. According to Article 1, Section 12 of the California State Constitution,

> A person shall be released on bail by sufficient sureties, except for:
>
> (a) Capital crimes when the facts are evident or the presumption great;
> (b) Felony offenses involving acts of violence on another person, or felony sexual assault offenses on another person, when the facts are evident or the presumption great and the court finds based upon clear and convincing evidence that there is a substantial likelihood the person's release would result in great bodily harm to others; or
> (c) Felony offenses when the facts are evident or the presumption great and the court finds based on clear and convincing evidence that the person has threatened another with great bodily harm and that there is a substantial likelihood that the person would carry out the threat if released.
>
> Excessive bail may not be required. In fixing the amount of bail, the court shall take into consideration the seriousness of the offense charged, the previous criminal record of the defendant, and the probability of his or her appearing at the trial or hearing of the case.
>
> A person may be released on his or her own recognizance in the court's discretion.

The court has a number of options when setting conditions of pretrial release. These include:

- payment of cash bail in exchange for pretrial release;
- payment of non-cash bail (usually a property bond where the defendant deposits some form of property as collateral for release);
- release on personal recognizance (where the defendant is released without any bail); and
- conditional release (where the defendant is required as a condition of pretrial release to attend a treatment or other program).

In many cases, the defendant will also be asked to make an initial **plea** to the charges at the arraignment. At this time, the defendant will also be asked to plead to the charges. Most defendants will plead either guilty or not guilty. In some cases, defendants will plead *nolo contendere*, which indicates that they "do not contest" the charges. The plea of *nolo contendere* is most commonly used when there is a civil trial pending and the proceedings and outcome of a criminal trial may be used in the civil trial. Once a plea of *nolo contendere* is made, it must be accepted by the court and the results of the criminal trial cannot be used against the defendant in a civil trial.

If a defendant is charged with a felony and pleads not guilty, a preliminary hearing must be held. In addition, PC §1049.5 requires that the trial date be no more than 60 days from the date of the defendant's arraignment in superior court unless the court lengthens the time for good cause.

Preliminary Hearing

Only those defendants who have been charged with a felony offense are required to have a **preliminary hearing.** Unless the defendant waives his or her right to a preliminary hearing, the hearing must occur within ten days of the arraignment and, according to PC §1043.5, the defendant must be personally present. The primary purpose of a preliminary hearing (or the alternative step, a **grand jury indictment**) is to make certain that defendants are brought to trial only if there is sufficient evidence against them. During the preliminary hearing, the district attorney presents evidence to show that there is probable cause to believe both that a crime was committed and that the defendant committed it. If the judge determines that the district attorney has not shown sufficient evidence, the charges are dropped and the defendant is released. If the judge determines that there is sufficient evidence to bring the defendant to trial, the defendant will be "held to answer" to the charges in the Superior Court.

California's preliminary hearing is unusual. In most states, the preliminary hearing may last only a few hours. However, in California, the preliminary hearing is an extremely detailed and in-depth procedure that may last several weeks. Fans of old television programs, who remember the courtroom scenes in *Perry Mason*, may recall that juries were never present during Perry Mason's dramatic speeches proving his clients' innocence. That is because those scenes were always set in the preliminary hearing phase of the court proceedings, not during an actual criminal trial.

Plea Bargaining

While plea bargaining is not a formal stage of the criminal justice process, it is an extremely important process in every state, including California. Over 90 percent of all felony and misdemeanor convictions in California are the result of guilty pleas. PC §1192.7(b) defines plea bargaining in California as:

> any bargaining, negotiation, or discussion between a criminal defendant, or his or her counsel, and a prosecuting attorney or judge, whereby the defendant agrees to plead guilty or nolo contendere, in exchange for any promises, commitments, concessions, assurances, or consideration by the prosecuting attorney or judge relating to any charge against the defendant or to the sentencing of the defendant.

In 1982, California voters passed Proposition 8, also known as the *Victims' Bill of Rights*. One of the elements in this bill significantly affected the use of plea bargaining in California. As a result of the passage of Proposition 8, PC §1192.7(a) states that plea bargaining may not be used in any case in which the indictment or information charge involves a serious felony or a felony in which the defendant used a firearm, or in any offense involving driving under the influence of an intoxicating substance, except in the following situations:

- There is insufficient evidence to prove the people's case,
- The testimony of a material witness cannot be obtained
- A reduction or dismissal would not result in a substantial change in the sentence received by the defendant

During the plea bargaining process, the prosecutor negotiates with the defense attorney and/or the defendant. The purpose of the negotiation is to reach an agreement whereby the defendant will enter a plea of guilty to a charge (either the original charge or a lesser or related charge.) In exchange for this plea, the prosecutor may do one or more of the following:

- drop any other charges which have been filed against the defendant;
- make recommendations to the court concerning sentencing (although these recommendations are not binding on the trial judge);
- agree not to oppose the defendant's request for a certain sentence (although this request is not binding on the trial judge); or
- agree to a specific sentence.

The defense attorney is responsible for advising the defendant of all plea offers and any other relevant matters that may affect the defendant's decision (e.g., the possible results of each plea). The defense attorney may not accept any plea bargain without the full consent of the defendant. While the trial judge does not participate directly in plea bargaining, the judge is still an important element in the process because he/she must accept the plea.

Discovery

After the charging document has been filed, the defense has the opportunity to engage in the **discovery process**, obtaining additional information about the prosecution's case and by inspecting any physical evidence possessed by the prosecutor. The discovery process is discussed in PC §1054 through 1054.9. According to PC §1054, the purposes of the discovery process include:

(a) To promote the ascertainment of truth in trials by requiring timely pretrial discovery.
(b) To save court time by requiring that discovery be conducted informally between and among the parties before judicial enforcement is requested.
(c) To save court time in trial and avoid the necessity for frequent interruptions and postponements.

(d) To protect victims and witnesses from danger, harassment, and undue delay of the proceedings.
(e) To provide that no discovery shall occur in criminal cases except as provided by this chapter, other express statutory provisions, or as mandated by the Constitution of the United States.

Disclosure of information must be made at least 30 days before the date of trial.[29] California's discovery process is reciprocal. This means that not only must the prosecution provide the defendant with information, but the defense also is required to provide certain information to the prosecution. PC §1054.1 outlines the information that the prosecution must provide to the defense and PC §1054.3 specifies the information that the defense must disclose to the prosecution.

Trial

Less than ten percent of all felony and misdemeanor cases go to a formal criminal **trial**; the vast majority are disposed of by a plea of guilty on the part of the defendant. If the defendant enters a plea of not guilty and the case does go to trial, the procedure is essentially the same regardless of whether the case involves a felony or a misdemeanor.

According to both the Sixth Amendment to the U.S. Constitution and Article I, Section 15 of the California State Constitution, all defendants have the right to a speedy and public trial. The California State Constitution also guarantees the right to a **jury trial** in all criminal cases.[30] If the defendant is charged with a felony, the jury will be made of 12 individuals; in misdemeanor cases, the jury may consist of fewer than 12 jurors if both parties agree in open court.[31] A defendant may waive his or her right to a jury trial with the court's approval. In these cases, the defendant will be given a **bench trial**.

The basic steps involved in a trial in California are outlined in PC 1093.

Jury Selection

The first step in a trial is the selection of the jury. Trial juries for criminal cases in California are selected in the same manner as trial juries for civil actions.[32] Because of this, the procedure for the selection of juries is discussed in the California Code of Civil Procedure (CCP), rather than in the California Penal Code. Most trial juries include twelve persons, although if the trial is expected to be a long one, alternate jurors may also be selected. Original and alternate jurors are drawn from the same source and selected in the same manner.[33] CCP §197(b) states that there are two appropriate source lists for juror selection in California: the list of registered voters and the Department of Motor Vehicles' list of licensed drivers and identification cardholders who are resident within the area served by the court. According to CCP §203(a), all individuals are eligible and qualified to be prospective jurors, with the following exceptions:

- non-U.S. citizens
- individuals under 18 years of age
- individuals not legally resident in California
- individuals not resident in the jurisdiction in which they are summoned to serve

- individuals who have been convicted of a felony or of malfeasance in office and who have not had their civil rights restored
- individuals who do not have sufficient knowledge of the English language
- individuals currently serving on a grand jury or trial jury in any court in California
- individuals who are the subject of conservatorship

In addition, CCP §219 exempts peace officers from jury selection in criminal trials.

The process of jury selection is known as ***voir dire*** and involves an examination of the prospective jurors by the court and by the attorneys for both the prosecution and the defense. The stated purpose of the *voir dire* is to determine whether each potential juror is impartial and will be able to render a fair verdict in a case. Potential jurors are placed under oath and then questioned by the judge, prosecutor, and defense counsel.

During the process, both the defense and the district attorneys are allowed to make challenges, or to object to the inclusion of certain potential trial jurors. California allows two types of challenges to prospective jurors.[34] **Challenges for cause** generally are based on the attorney's belief that the juror is biased in some way that will prevent him or her from acting impartially and without prejudice during the trial. **Peremptory challenges** may be used by either attorney to remove potential jurors from the jury panel without giving specific reasons. If the offense to which the defendant is charged is punishable by death or life imprisonment, the defense and the state are each entitled to twenty peremptory challenges. In most other cases, each is entitled to ten peremptory challenges. However, if the offense charged is punishable by a maximum term of imprisonment of 90 days or less, the defense and the state are each entitled to only six peremptory challenges.[35]

After the selection of the jury is completed, the jurors are sworn in by the court. CCP §232(b) specifies the oath of trial jurors, which is acknowledged by the statement, "I do":

> "Do you and each of you understand and agree that you will well and truly try the cause now pending before this court, and a true verdict render according only to the evidence presented to you and to the instructions of the court."

The Charge

Once the jury is selected and sworn in, the trial itself begins. If the charged offense is a felony, the court clerk reads the charge to the jury and states the defendant's plea. This step is omitted if the defendant is not charged with a felony offense.[36]

Opening Statements

Both the prosecutor and the defense attorney are entitled to make an opening statement which provides all the participants in the trial, especially the jury, with an overview of the facts of the case. In California, the district attorney makes the first statement. After the prosecution's opening remarks are completed, the defense may make an opening statement immediately or may choose to wait until after the prosecutor has introduced the evidence in support of the charge.[37]

Presentation of the Prosecution's Evidence

After the opening statements are completed, the prosecution begins to present evidence in support of the charge that has been brought against the defendant. The prosecution presents first because the state is bringing the charge against the defendant and, because of the presumption of innocence, has assumed the burden of proof. Evidence submitted into court may include be pictures, documents, recordings, depositions, objects, or sworn testimony by witnesses. The judge determines the admissibility of each piece of evidence, based on the rules set forth in the California Evidence Code (EC). EC §351 states that, "Except as otherwise provided by statute, all relevant evidence is admissible." These rules are primarily intended to ensure that unreliable evidence, or evidence that was illegally obtained, is not received in court.

The district attorney generally begins with **direct examination** of the prosecution's first witness, who is obviously expected to give evidence to support the state's case against the defendant. After the district attorney finishes questioning the witness, the defense is allowed to **cross-examine** the same witness. If the prosecutor wishes, he/she may then return to ask the witness more questions in a process known as **re-direct examination**. Following this, the defense attorney has the option to question the witness once more during the **re-cross examination**. This procedure is repeated for each witness called by the prosecution.

Presentation of the Defense's Evidence

After the prosecution has presented all its evidence and called all its witnesses, the defense may offer evidence.[38] Generally, the defense begins by putting forth a motion to dismiss all charges or to acquit, on the grounds that the evidence offered by the prosecution was insufficient. If the motion is denied, the defense presents its evidence.

If the defense attorney chose not to make an opening statement at the start of the trial, he/she may make one now. The defense then proceeds to present its evidence. The procedure for the presentation of the evidence by the defense is similar to that of the prosecution: direct examination, cross examination, re-direct, and re-cross. The defendant is not required to testify at any point in the trial; both the U.S. Constitution and the California State Constitution protect the defendant against self-incrimination.

Rebuttal and Surrebuttal

After the defense has presented its evidence, each side may be given the opportunity to offer rebutting testimony or evidence. First, the prosecutor may present a **rebuttal**, including additional evidence that may nullify or challenge that presented by the defense. Then the defense is given the opportunity to present a **surrebuttal** case.[39]

Closing Arguments

Once all the evidence is presented, each side is given the opportunity to make a **closing argument**. During this stage of the trial, each attorney reviews and summarizes the evidence that best supports his/her side of the case, discusses any inferences that may be drawn from that evidence, and points out weaknesses in the opponent's case. In California, the prosecution makes its closing arguments first, followed by the defense. The prosecution is then given a final opportunity for rebuttal, thus the prosecution both opens and closes the final arguments in the trial.[40]

Instructions to the Jury

After the final closing arguments are completed, the judge has the opportunity to provide instructions to the jury regarding any legal issues or points of law which are applicable to the case and which the jury must follow when deciding on a verdict. This step is also known as **charging the jury**. During this stage, the judge may review the testimony presented in the trial and may make any comments on the evidence and on the testimony and credibility of witnesses that he/she feels is necessary for the proper determination of the case. The judge may also state the law applicable to the case, including defining the offense(s) with which the defendant is charged, discussing legal defenses to a crime, reminding the jury about the presumption of innocence, clarifying the meaning of burden of proof, and reviewing the concept of reasonable doubt.[41] *California Jury Instructions - Criminal* (CALJIC) is a published work which contains a set of standard instructions used by judges in California to instruct the jury regarding legal issues.

Jury Deliberation and Verdict Rendition

After the judge has given instructions to the jury, the jury may either decide in court or may retire to the jury room for **deliberation**.[42] The jurors discuss the case and attempt to come to agreement on a verdict concerning the guilt or innocence of the defendant. California law requires that all twelve jurors agree on a guilty verdict before the defendant can be convicted of the charge. If the jurors are unable to agree on a verdict after a reasonable period of time, they are **deadlocked** and considered to be a "**hung jury**". If this happens, the judge will declare a **mistrial** and the case may have to be retried in front of a new jury.

If the jurors come to an agreement on a **verdict**, they are returned to the courtroom and the verdict is read in open court. Either the defense or the prosecution is entitled to request a poll of the jury to ensure that each member of the jury agrees with the verdict and that no member was coerced or intimidated into agreeing, or agreed simply out of exhaustion. If any juror responds negatively, the court must refuse to accept the verdict and direct the jury to resume deliberations.

If the verdict of the jury is not guilty, the trial is over and the defendant is free to go. Because of the constitutional protection against double jeopardy, the defendant may never be retried on the same charges. The trial court judge is required to accept a verdict of not guilty. However, if the defendant is found guilty, the judge may still acquit the defendant if the judge believes that the evidence did not prove the defendant's guilt beyond a reasonable doubt.

If the defendant has waived his or her right to a jury trial, the trial court judge or justice pronounces the verdict at the conclusion of the trial.[43]

Proceedings Between the Verdict and the Sentence

If the defendant is found guilty, he/she will be sentenced. However, after a verdict of guilty is rendered and before the sentencing phase of the trial, the defendant may make a **post-trial motion** to set aside or modify the verdict. If the judge sets aside the verdict, the defendant may be entitled to a dismissal, a reduction of the charges, or a new trial. These motions are rarely granted.

The Sentence

In a felony case, if the defendant is found guilty, the judge must schedule a **sentencing hearing** within 20 judicial days after the verdict.[44] The California Penal Code specifies punishments for each crime. The maximum possible sentence depends on the level of the offense: for an infraction, the maximum sentence is a fine, for a misdemeanor, the maximum sentence is up to one year in a county jail, and for a felony, it is incarceration for at least one year in a state prison or, for murder with special circumstances, death. Some counties also offer diversion programs that allow the judge to order the defendant to go to counseling, get medical treatment, or perform some type of community service work. For certain types of misdemeanor and felony charges, the diversion may replace a fine or a sentence of incarceration. The sentencing process is discussed in more detail in the next chapter.

Appeal

If the defendant is convicted of a crime, he/she may have the option of **appealing** the conviction. Defendants are entitled to appeal if all post-trial motions were denied by the judge at the trial. In some cases, the prosecution may also have the right to appeal a verdict of not guilty, although this is a much less common occurrence. An appeal does not involve retrying a case or even re-examining the factual issues surrounding the crime; it only involves an examination or review of the legal issues involved in the case. The purpose of an appeal is to make certain that the defendant received a fair trial and that he/she was not deprived of any constitutional rights at any time.

NOTES

1. 28 U.S.C. 84
2. 28 U.S.C. 41
3. See California State Constitution of 1849, Article 6
4. California State Constitution, Article 6, Section 15
5. California State Constitution, Article 6, Section 10
6. California State Constitution, Article 6, Section 12
7. California State Constitution, Article 6, Section 11
8. PC §1239(b)
9. *The Supreme Court of California, 2003 edition* (www.courtinfo.ca.gov/courts/supreme)
10. *Ibid*
11. California Courts of Appeal (http://www.courtinfo.ca.gov/courts/courtsofappeal/about.htm)
12. California State Constitution, Article 6, Section 16(a)
13. California State Constitution, Article 6, Section 15
14. California State Constitution, Article 6, Section 10
15. California State Constitution, Article 6, Section 16
16. California State Constitution, Article 6, Section 6
17. *Ibid*
18. California State Courts: Judicial Council Activities (http://www.courtinfo.ca.gov/courtadmin/jc/activities.htm)
19. California State Constitution, Article 6, Section 7
20. California State Constitution, Article 6, Section 8 and 18
21. State of California Commission on Judicial Performance home page (http://cjp.ca.gov/)
22. California State Courts: Commission on Judicial Performance (http://www.courtinfo.ca.gov/courtadmin/otheragencies.htm)
23. California State Constitution, Article 6, Section 8
24. State Bar of California home page (http://www.calbar.ca.gov/)
25. *The State Bar of California: What Does It Do? How Does It Work?* (http://www.calbar.ca.gov/calbar/pdfs/whowhat1.pdf)

26. PC §834
27. PC §825(a)(1)
28. *Stack v. Boyle*, 342 U.S. 1 (1951)
29. PC §1054.7
30. California State Constitution, Article 1, Section 16
31. *Ibid*
32. PC §1046
33. CCP §234
34. CCP §225(b)
35. CCP §231
36. PC §1093(a)
37. PC §1093(b)
38. PC §1093(c)
39. PC §1903(d)
40. PC §1093(e)
41. PC §1093(f)
42. PC §1128
43. PC §1167
44. PC §1191

CHAPTER 6

SENTENCING IN CALIFORNIA

INTRODUCTION

After a criminal defendant pleads guilty or is found guilty in court by a judge or jury, the judge must impose a **sentence** of punishment upon the offender. Rule 4.410 of the 2003 *California Rules of Court*[1] sets forth seven general objectives in sentencing which are intended to guide the sentencing judge. These include:

(a) Protecting society.
(b) Punishing the defendant.
(c) Encouraging the defendant to lead a law abiding life in the future and deterring him from future offenses.
(d) Deterring others from criminal conduct by demonstrating its consequences.
(e) Preventing the defendant from committing new crimes by isolating him for the period of incarceration.
(f) Securing restitution for the victims of crime.
(g) Achieving uniformity in sentencing.

The Rule states out that these objectives may at times conflict with one another, so that an attempt to meet one objective may make it difficult, or even impossible to also meet another objective. When this occurs, the sentencing judge must make a decision based on the individual case at hand as to which objectives have a higher priority.

Rule 4.410 also states that "the sentencing judge should be guided by statutory statements of policy, the criteria in these rules, and the facts and circumstances of the case." However, it is clearly possible for a judge also to be influenced by various extra-legal factors, including the judge's own personal biases, beliefs, and characteristics.

In some contrast to the seven objectives outlined in the *California Rules of Court*, PC §1170(a)(1) clearly states that "The Legislature finds and declares that the purpose of imprisonment for crime is punishment." This statement was reaffirmed by the California Supreme Court in the case of *People v. Warner*.[2]

TYPES OF SENTENCES

A variety of sentences may be imposed upon convicted offenders in California. Sentences acceptable in the California courts include:

- fines

- restitution
- probation
- other community-based or intermediate sanctions (e.g., boot camp, house arrest with electronic monitoring, shock incarceration)
- imprisonment (in a jail or a prison)
- death

Combinations of these sentences are also allowed. For example, a judge may order both imprisonment and a fine, or order the offender to pay a fine as well as victim restitution.

The judge does not have total discretion as to the sentence imposed; the California Penal Code outlines the appropriate sentences for each specific offense. It is possible for a judge to impose a combination of several sentences. For example, according to PC §490, the punishment for petty theft is a fine of up to $1,000 or a jail sentence of up to six months, or both. Thus, under this statute, the judge is free to sentence the offender to either a fine or imprisonment, or to require the offender to pay a fine and serve jail time as well. However, the judge is not free to sentence the offender to a term of imprisonment greater than six months or impose a fine of more than $1,000.

WHEN SENTENCING OCCURS

If a defendant enters a plea of guilty at the arraignment, there is no trial and the court proceeds directly to the sentencing phase. Defendants who plead guilty to a misdemeanor charge may be sentenced at the arraignment, unless the judge chooses to postpone sentencing and order the probation department to prepare a pre-sentencing report. If the defendant pleads guilty to a felony charge at the arraignment, he/she waives the right to a trial and proceeds to the sentencing phase of the criminal court procedures.

If the defendant enters a plea of not guilty and is then found guilty in a criminal trial, the sentence may be imposed by the court immediately following the trial or in a sentencing hearing scheduled for a later date. If the crime for which the offender has been found guilty is a misdemeanor, the offender may be sentenced immediately following the jury's presentation of the verdict. However, if the jury reaches a guilty verdict in a felony case, the judge will order the probation department to prepare a pre-sentencing report and schedule a hearing. According to PC §1191, the sentencing hearing must be scheduled no more than 20 judicial days after the conclusion of the trial.

DETERMINATE AND INDETERMINATE SENTENCING

A **determinate sentence** is a flat or fixed-term prison sentence for an offense, while a sentence that includes a range of time between a specified minimum and maximum is known as an **indeterminate sentence**. In other words, an indeterminate sentence includes a range of time to be served in prison (for example, three- to- five years in the state prison) and a determinate sentence is a fixed period of time (for example, four years in prison).

In 1917, California passed the **Indeterminate Sentencing Act**. Prior to the passage of this Act, the trial judge had full authority to determine the length of sentence for offenses that were punishable by imprisonment in a state prison. The Act changed this, giving the authority to fix the length of a prison sentence to an administrative agency known as the Adult Authority. While the Act was in force, California courts emphasized the use of indeterminate sentences. The purpose of the use of indeterminate sentences was an attempt to make the punishment better fit the crime and to focus more attention on the individual inmate's potential rehabilitation.

However, in 1976, California became one of the first states to enact fixed-term sentencing legislation with the passage of the **Determinate Sentencing Act.** This Act repealed the Indeterminate Sentencing Act, which now applies only to individuals serving sentences for crimes committed prior to July 1, 1977. The goals of the Determinate Sentencing Act include consistency, equity, and simplicity of sentencing. According to PC §1170(a)(1),

> The Legislature finds and declares that the purpose of imprisonment for crime is punishment. This purpose is best served by terms proportionate to the seriousness of the offense with provision for uniformity in the sentences of offenders committing the same offense under similar circumstances. The Legislature further finds and declares that the elimination of disparity and the provision of uniformity of sentences can best be achieved by determinate sentences fixed by statute in proportion to the seriousness of the offense as determined by the Legislature to be imposed by the court with specified discretion.

Basically, the Act states that if the court hands down a sentence that includes a term of incarceration in a state prison, the exact term of that imprisonment must be specified. Indeterminate sentences are, with a few exceptions, no longer used in the state. The acceptable sentence for a crime is stated in the statute.

Some statutes actually state three different terms of imprisonment as acceptable sentences for a specific crime. For example, PC §461 states that first degree burglary is punishable by imprisonment in the state prison for two, four, or six years. In these situations, the court is required to impose the middle term, or **midterm**, unless there are aggravating or mitigating circumstances. For the crime of first degree burglary, the midterm is four years in a state prison. If there are aggravating factors present in the commission of the offense (for example, if the offender used a weapon in the commission of the crime), the court may impose the upper, or **aggravated term** of six years in a state prison. If there are mitigating circumstances present (for example, if this is the offender's first offense), the judge may order the lower, or **mitigated term** of two years.[3]

There are several exceptions to the use of determinate sentences in California. One example is the **three-strikes law**[4], which mandates a sentence of 25 years to life for offenders convicted of a third felony. Therefore, an offender sentenced under the three-strikes law is effectively given a minimum sentence of 25 years and a maximum sentence of life in prison. In addition, the California Penal Code does specify some indeterminate sentences. For example, according to PC §190(a), an individual convicted of second degree murder is to be punished by imprisonment in the state prison for a term of 15 years to life; essentially a minimum sentence of 15 years and a maximum sentence of life in prison. The Penal Code also states that some violent crimes are punishable by a sentence of life imprisonment with the possibility of parole after a set period of time. For example, an individual convicted of aggravated arson may be punished by imprisonment in the state prison for a period of ten years to life, and will not be eligible for parole release for at least ten years.[5] This sentence is indeterminate because the offender is eligible for parole after a minimum period of time but is not guaranteed parole. If an offender is granted parole, he/she serves the minimum time. However, if the offender is denied parole, he/she will have to serve longer than the minimum sentence.

AGGRAVATING AND MITIGATING CIRCUMSTANCES

Rules 4.421 and 4.423 of the *California Rules of Court* outline a series of aggravating and mitigating circumstances which allow the sentencing judge to depart to some extent from the specific determinate sentence outlined in the penal code. **Aggravating circumstances** are factors about the crime or the offender that increase the seriousness of the crime or make it worse than usual in some way. **Mitigating circumstances** are factors that make a crime less serious in some way. According to Rule 4.421, aggravating circumstances include:

(a) Facts relating to the crime, whether or not charged or chargeable as enhancements, including the fact that:
- (1) The crime involved great violence, great bodily harm, threat of great bodily harm, or other acts disclosing a high degree of cruelty, viciousness, or callousness.
- (2) The defendant was armed with or used a weapon at the time of the commission of the crime.
- (3) The victim was particularly vulnerable.
- (4) The defendant induced others to participate in the commission of the crime or occupied a position of leadership or dominance of other participants in its commission.
- (5) The defendant induced a minor to commit or assist in the commission of the crime.
- (6) The defendant threatened witnesses, unlawfully prevented or dissuaded witnesses from testifying, suborned perjury, or in any other way illegally interfered with the judicial process.
- (7) The defendant was convicted of other crimes for which consecutive sentences could have been imposed but for which concurrent sentences are being imposed.
- (8) The manner in which the crime was carried out indicates planning, sophistication, or professionalism.
- (9) The crime involved an attempted or actual taking or damage of great monetary value.
- (10) The crime involved a large quantity of contraband.
- (11) The defendant took advantage of a position of trust or confidence to commit the offense.

(b) Facts relating to the defendant, including the fact that:
- (1) The defendant has engaged in violent conduct which indicates a serious danger to society.

   (2) The defendant's prior convictions as an adult or sustained petitions in juvenile delinquency proceedings are numerous or of increasing seriousness.
   (3) The defendant has served a prior prison term.
   (4) The defendant was on probation or parole when the crime was committed.
   (5) The defendant's prior performance on probation or parole was unsatisfactory.

(c) Any other facts statutorily declared to be circumstances in aggravation.

The presence of one or more of these circumstances may require the judge to impose the upper, or aggravated term, in situations where the statute lists three possible terms of imprisonment.

Rule 4.423 lists the mitigating circumstances which may be considered by the court, including:

(a) Facts relating to the crime, including the fact that:
   (1) The defendant was a passive participant or played a minor role in the crime.
   (2) The victim was an initiator of, willing participant in, or aggressor or provoker of the incident.
   (3) The crime was committed because of an unusual circumstance, such as great provocation, which is unlikely to recur.
   (4) The defendant participated in the crime under circumstances of coercion or duress, or the criminal conduct was partially excusable for some other reason not amounting to a defense.
   (5) The defendant, with no apparent predisposition to do so, was induced by others to participate in the crime.
   (6) The defendant exercised caution to avoid harm to persons or damage to property, or the amounts of money or property taken were deliberately small, or no harm was done or threatened against the victim.
   (7) The defendant believed that he or she had a claim or right to the property taken, or for other reasons mistakenly believed that the conduct was legal.
   (8) The defendant was motivated by a desire to provide necessities for his or her family or self.
   (9) The defendant suffered from repeated or continuous physical, sexual, or psychological abuse inflicted by the victim of the crime; and the victim of the crime, who inflicted the abuse, was the defendant's spouse, intimate cohabitant, or parent of the defendant's child; and the facts concerning the abuse do not amount to a defense.

(b) Facts relating to the defendant, including the fact that:
   (1) The defendant has no prior record, or an insignificant record of criminal conduct, considering the recency and frequency of prior crimes.
   (2) The defendant was suffering from a mental or physical condition that significantly reduced culpability for the crime.

(3) The defendant voluntarily acknowledged wrongdoing prior to arrest or at an early stage of the criminal process.
(4) The defendant is ineligible for probation and but for that ineligibility would have been granted probation.
(5) The defendant made restitution to the victim.
(6) The defendant's prior performance on probation or parole was satisfactory.

The presence of mitigating circumstances may allow the judge to impose the lower, or mitigated term, in situations where the statute lists three possible terms of imprisonment.

According to Rule 4.420 of the *California Rules of Court*, aggravating and mitigating circumstances are established by a preponderance of evidence, rather than by proof beyond a reasonable doubt. If both aggravating and mitigating circumstances exist, the judge may only impose the upper term if, after all the relevant facts are considered (e.g., the case record, the probation officer's report, evidence presented at the sentencing hearing), the aggravating circumstances are found to outweigh the mitigating circumstances. Similarly, the judge is only justified in imposing the lower term if the mitigating circumstances are found to outweigh the aggravating circumstances.

The issue of aggravating circumstances is particularly important in the crime of first degree murder, because the death penalty can only be imposed for this crime when certain special or aggravating circumstances are present. These include factors such as the use of torture or the killing of multiple victims. This topic is discussed in more detail in Chapter 7.

CONCURRENT VERSUS CONSECUTIVE SENTENCES

If an offender is convicted of multiple offenses, the court must impose a sentence for each offense. If the sentences imposed involve terms of imprisonment in either a county jail or a state prison, the court has the option of requiring the sentences to be served concurrently or consecutively. **Concurrent sentences** are served at the same time while **consecutive sentences** are served in succession, one after the other. For example, if an offender is convicted of two counts of first degree burglary and receives midterm sentences of four years in a state prison for each count, to be served concurrently, both sentences are satisfied after a total of four years. If, however, the sentences are to be served consecutively, the offender must serve a total of eight years to satisfy both sentences.

Rule 4.425 of the *California Rules of Court* outlines a set of criteria that affect the decision as to whether the imposed sentences shall be concurrent or consecutive. Some of these criteria relate specifically to the crime committed, including:

- whether the crimes and their objectives were predominantly independent of each other (rather than all the crimes being incident to one objective)

- whether the crimes involved separate acts or threats of violence

- whether the crimes were committed at different times or separate places (rather than being committed close together in time and place, which could indicate one period of aberrant behavior)

In other words, if two or more crimes were committed during one event or were incident to one objective, and the offender is convicted of these crimes, the sentences that are imposed must be served concurrently. If, on the other hand, the offender committed the crimes separately (for example, the offender robbed several gas stations over a period of two months), and is convicted of multiple crimes, the court may order that the sentences be served consecutively.

In addition, the Rule states that aggravating or mitigating circumstances may be considered by the court when making the decision whether to impose consecutive rather than concurrent sentences. However, there are several exceptions to this. Circumstances which may not be considered include:

- a fact that is used to impose the upper or aggravated term
- a fact that is used to otherwise enhance the offender's prison sentence
- a fact that is an element of the crime

The rationale behind excluding these facts from consideration is that they have already been used against the offender in the determination of the length of the sentence and may not be used a second time to enhance the sentence length by requiring consecutive sentences.

INTERMEDIATE SENTENCES

Intermediate (or alternative) sentences are punishments that are harsher than probation but less punitive than a prison sentence. California began to serious emphasize the use of intermediate sanctions with the passage of the California Community-Based Punishment Act in 1994. Community-based punishment programs specifically target non-violent offenders[6] and emphasize reducing the populations of local jails to increase the space available for other offenders, such as new admissions, and parole and probation violators.[7] According to PC §8051(b), community-based programs must not only punish offenders but also provide the offenders with opportunities to change their behavior.

PC §8052(e) defines the concept of "intermediate sanction" and lists a variety of intermediate sanctions which may be used:

> "Intermediate sanctions" means punishment options and sanctions other than simple incarceration in prison or jail or traditional routine probation supervision. Intermediate sanctions may be provided by correctional agencies directly or through community-based public or private correctional service providers, and include, but are not limited to, the following:

(1) Short-term "shock" incarceration in either jail or prison, for a period of not more than 60 days.
(2) Incarceration in a "boot camp" facility.
(3) Intensive supervision.
(4) Home detention with electronic monitoring.
(5) Mandatory community service.
(6) Restorative justice programs such as mandatory victim restitution and victim-offender reconciliation.
(7) Work, training, or education in a furlough program...
(8) Work, in lieu of confinement, in a work release program...
(9) Day reporting.
(10) Mandatory residential or nonresidential substance abuse treatment programs...
(11) Mandatory random drug testing.
(12) Mother-infant care programs.
(13) Community-based residential programs offering structure, supervision, drug treatment, alcohol treatment, literacy programming, employment counseling, psychological counseling, or any combination of these and other interventions.

Community-based punishments are administered by the California Board of Corrections in partnership with county government and community-based private and public correctional service providers.

VICTIM RIGHTS AND SERVICES

Victim Impact Statements

Victim impact statements are written reports or verbal statements that are given to the sentencing judge and that describe the effects of the crime upon the victim. In California, Rule 4.411.5 of the *California Rules of Court* requires that the presentence investigation report, which is prepared by the probation department before the sentencing hearing, must include a victim impact statement. Through this statement, victims are given the opportunity to provide the court with information on the impact that the crime has had upon their lives, including factors such as property loss, physical injury, emotional injury, and out-of-pocket expenses incurred as a result of the crime.

In California, victims are not required to personally attend the sentencing hearing but if they wish to attend, they have the right to do so. They also have the right to make a victim impact statement at felony sentencing hearings and parole hearings. This is known as the **right of allocution**. During this statement, victims may speak on matters concerning the crime, the penalty, and the need for restitution. They may express their views of the defendant, the crime, and any other relevant facts and circumstances. According to PC 1191.1,

> The victim, or up to two of the victim's parents or guardians if the victim is a minor, or the next of kin of the victim if the victim has died, have the right to appear, personally or by counsel, at the sentencing proceeding and to reasonably express

> his, her, or their views concerning the crime, the person responsible, and the need for restitution. The court in imposing sentence shall consider the statements of victims, parents or guardians, and next of kin made pursuant to this section and shall state on the record its conclusion concerning whether the person would pose a threat to public safety if granted probation.

The victim (or his or her parents or next of kin) does not have to be physically present at the sentencing hearing to exercise his or her right of allocution. PC §1191.15 grants victims the right to submit a statement in writing, on audiotape, or on videotape if they so choose.

The probation department is required by law[8] to notify victims, or their next of kin, of all sentencing proceedings for felony cases. The victim also has the right to know the sentence the probation officer will recommend to the court, although he/she is not entitled to inspect the actual probation report prior to sentencing. Making a statement at a sentencing or parole hearing may be valuable to victims because it enables them to take an active role in the criminal justice process.

The Right to Restitution

Restitution generally involves requiring the offender to pay a sum of money to the victim as reimbursement for economic losses due to the crime. Restitution may also be in a nonmonetary form. According to the California State Constitution, "all persons who suffer losses as a result of criminal activity shall have the right to restitution from the persons convicted of the crimes for losses they suffer."[9] Similarly, PC §1202.4(a)(1) states that "It is the intent of the Legislature that a victim of crime who incurs any economic loss as a result of the commission of a crime shall receive restitution directly from any defendant convicted of that crime."

The court is required to consider ordering the defendant to make restitution, in addition to any other punishment that may be imposed, unless there is a compelling reason not to do so.[10] Thus, restitution may be ordered even if the judge sentences the offender to a fine or a term of imprisonment in jail or prison.

Restitution only applies to economic losses that result from the defendant's criminal actions. According to PC §1202.4(f)(3), economic losses that may be eligible for restitution include, but are not limited to:

- the cost of replacing or repairing stolen or damaged property
- medical expenses
- mental health counseling expenses
- wages or profits lost because of injury to the victim
- wages or profits lost because of time the victim spent as a witness or assisting the police or prosecution
- attorney's fees
- the cost of the victim relocating away from the defendant, if relocation is deemed necessary by the police or by a mental health treatment provider
- the cost of installing or increasing residential security as the result of the crime

- the cost of retrofitting a residence and/or vehicle to make them accessible if the victim is permanently disabled as a result of the crime

The Right to Compensation

In addition to restitution, victims may be eligible for **victim compensation**. While restitution is paid to the victim by the convicted offender, restitution is paid to the victim by the state. According to Government Code (GC) §13950(a),

> The Legislature finds and declares that it is in the public interest to assist residents of the State of California in obtaining compensation for the pecuniary losses they suffer as a direct result of criminal acts.

The state agency responsible for dealing with victim compensation is the **California Victim Compensation and Government Claims Board**, which is composed of three members, including the Director of General Services, the State Controller, and a third member appointed by the governor.

GC §13955 outlines who is eligible to apply for compensation awards. Essentially, an individual is eligible for victim compensation from the state if:

- he/she suffered physical or emotional injury as the result of a violent crime
- he/she is a family member of a crime victim (parent, sibling, spouse, or child)
- he/she is a family member of the victim (including fiance) who witnessed the crime
- he/she pays for the medical and/or burial expenses of a deceased victim

In addition, the individual must meet a number of eligibility requirements, which include:

- the individual must be a resident of the state of California at the time of the crime, or be a nonresident who was in California at the time of the crime
- the individual must have reported the crime to the appropriate law enforcement agency and must cooperate in the investigation of the crime and the prosecution of any known suspect
- the individual may not have been involved or participated in the crime or the events leading up to it

Not all crimes are considered for compensation. In general, California only compensates victims of violent crimes, including but not limited to murder, sexual assault, robbery, vehicular manslaughter, assault with a deadly weapon, battery, child abuse, child molestation, domestic violence, and stalking.[11]

In addition, GC §13956 provides a list of individuals who are not eligible for victim compensation awards, including:

- the individual who committed the crime
- anyone who participated in the crime or was involved in the events leading up to the crime
- anyone who did not cooperate with the police in the investigation of the crime and/or anyone who did not cooperate with the district attorney in the prosecution of known suspects

Only certain expenses are eligible for reimbursement by the victim compensation program. These include (but are not limited to):

- medical and dental expenses
- mental health counseling
- lost wages and/or income
- lost support to eligible family members of the direct victim of the crime
- moving and relocation expenses for a victim of domestic violence
- funeral and burial expenses
- job retraining[12]

Personal property losses are not eligible for reimbursements, with the exception of certain medical-related property items (eyeglasses, hearing aids, prosthetic devices, etc.)[13]

All expenses must have been incurred as a direct result of a crime and no other source of reimbursement may be available. The victim compensation program is the victim's last resort. Thus, for example, if the victim has adequate health insurance, he/she may not request compensation for medical expenses that are covered by that insurance. In addition, if the victim receives restitution from the offender, he/she may not also receive victim compensation.

There are limits to the amount of compensation that may be received by a victim. According to the California Victim Compensation and Government Claims Board, the total compensation payable for a crime committed on or after January 1, 2001 cannot be more than $70,000. Several categories of expenses also have specific limitations. For example, a victim may be reimbursed for up to 75% of billed charges for in-patient hospital expenses. A direct victim, or each surviving family member of a deceased victim, may receive no more than $10,000 for outpatient mental health counseling expenses. Victims who were not permanently disabled as the result of the crime can only receive reimbursement of lost wages for up to five years. Compensation for funeral and burial expenses is limited to $5,000.

In most cases, applications for victim compensation for adult victims must be filed with the Board within one year of the crime. If the victim was a minor at the time of the crime, the application must be filed before the minor's 19th birthday. When the application is received by the Board, it is reviewed to determine if the applicant meets the criteria for eligibility. This process includes verifying all the information provided in the application and may involve interviewing witnesses, police, medical and mental health personnel, and employers. When the review process is complete, a written recommendation is made to approve or deny the claim. The process generally takes no more than 90 days (although it may take longer in some cases). If the applicant does not agree with the recommendation of the Board (generally this occurs if the Board recommends the claim be denied), there is an appeal process. The first step is for the applicant to request that the claim be discussed by the Board at a public hearing. If the applicant does not agree with the outcome of the public hearing, he/she may request that the Board reconsider its decision. To make such a request, the applicant must provide the Board with new and relevant information that has not previously been considered. Finally, an applicant who disagrees with the final decision of the Board may file a *writ of mandate* in the state superior court.

NOTES

1. *2003 California Rules of Court* (http://www.courtinfo.ca.gov/rules/)
2. *People v. Warner*, 20 Cal.3d 678, 143 Cal.Rptr. 885, 574 P.2d 1237 (1978)
3. PC §1170(b)
4. PC §667
5. PC §451.5(b) and (c)
6. PC §8051(d)
7. PC §8051(e)
8. PC §1191.1
9. California State Constitution, Article 1, Section 28(b)
10. PC §1202.4(b)
11. California Victim Compensation and Government Claims Board home page (http://www.boc.cahwnet.gov)
12. *Ibid*
13. GC §13957(a)(1)

CHAPTER 7

CAPITAL PUNISHMENT IN CALIFORNIA

THE HISTORY OF CAPITAL PUNISHMENT IN CALIFORNIA[1]

In California, the State Legislature authorized legal executions of convicted offenders under the Criminal Practices Act of 1851. **Capital punishment** was formally included in the Penal Code in 1872 at the county level. Executions were conducted by the county sheriff, whose presence was mandated by law at all executions, and were generally held within the confines of the county jail. The Legislature specifically forbade public executions, requiring that they be held in a convenient private place in the county. The method of execution used at this time was hanging.

In 1891, the Legislature passed an amendment which moved the death penalty to the state level. The new amendment required that executions be held inside one of the two existing state prisons, San Quentin or Folsom. The presence of the county sheriff was no longer required; he was replaced by the prison warden. The first state-conducted execution in California was held on March 3, 1893 at San Quentin and the first execution at Folsom was held on December 13, 1895. While there apparently was no official rule that judges followed when ordering offenders hanged at Folsom or San Quentin, it was customary to send recidivists to Folsom when a sentence of death was imposed.

Lethal gas replaced hanging as the method of execution used in California in 1937, although this new ruling did not affect those offenders who were already under a sentence of death. The last execution by hanging at Folsom was conducted on December 3, 1937 and the last hanging at San Quentin on May 1, 1942. In all, a total of 92 inmates were hanged at Folsom between 1895 and 1937 and 215 were hanged at San Quentin between 1893 and 1942. A lethal gas chamber was constructed at San Quentin in 1938 and was first used on December 2 of that year to execute two inmates. Between 1938 and 1967 a total of 194 persons were executed by lethal gas, including four women. The first woman to be executed in California was put to death in the gas chamber on November 21, 1941.

Executions in California continued until April 8, 1967. However, between 1967 and 1992, there were no executions in California, due to a variety of decisions by both the California Supreme Court and the United States Supreme Court. In February 1972, the California Supreme Court held that the death penalty constituted cruel and unusual punishment and thus violated the state and federal constitutions.[2] As a result of this ruling, the death sentences of 107 offenders were commuted. The same year, the voters approved Proposition 17 which sanctioned capital punishment, thus amending the state constitution and overruling the California Supreme Court. However, because of the U.S. Supreme Court's decision in *Furman v. Georgia*[3], which ruled that the death penalty, as it was administered, constituted "cruel and unusual punishment" and therefore was a violation of the Eighth Amendment of the U.S. Constitution, Proposition 17 did not revive the death penalty in California.

In response to *Furman*, legislation was passed in 1973 making the death penalty mandatory in certain cases and under certain conditions, including:

- kidnapping if the victim dies
- train wrecking if anyone dies
- assault by a prisoner serving a life sentence if the victim dies within one year of the assault
- treason against the state
- first degree murder with specific factors (murder for hire, murder of a peace officer, murder of a witness to prevent testimony, murder committed during a robbery, burglary, or rape by force, murder committed during the performance of lewd and lascivious acts upon children, and murder by a individual previously convicted of murder)

In 1976, the U.S. Supreme Court ruled in the case of *Gregg v. Georgia*[4] that capital punishment did not invariably violate the Constitution and reinstated the death penalty. Following this decision, the California Supreme Court unanimously ruled the California death penalty statute to be unconstitutional because the mandatory nature of the punishment did not allow the defendant to present any mitigating evidence.[5] This decision resulted in 70 inmates being taken off condemned status and re-sentenced.

In 1977, a new death penalty statute that allowed the defendant to present mitigating evidence was enacted by the Legislature. The statute reinstated the death penalty as a possible punishment for the crime of first degree murder when certain special circumstances were present. These included:

- murder for financial gain
- murder by an individual person previously convicted of murder
- murder of multiple victims
- murder involving torture
- murder of a peace officer
- murder of a witness to prevent testimony

The Legislature also revised the Penal Code to include a number of crimes that were punishable by either death or life imprisonment without the possibility of parole. These included treason, train derailing or wrecking, and securing the death of an innocent person through perjury. At the same time, the punishments for kidnapping, extortion, and robbery were changed from death to life without parole.

In 1978, in a state-wide election, the voters approved Proposition 7, a broader death penalty law that replaced the 1977 statutes. Proposition 7 expanded the list of special circumstances for which the death penalty could be imposed and changed the way aggravating and mitigating circumstances are considered in capital cases. The list of special circumstances was again enlarged in 1990. This is the death penalty statute under which the state currently operates. However, although Proposition 7 passed in 1978, another 14 years passed before anyone was again put to death in California. The first California execution in 25 years was held on April 21, 1992 when Robert Alton Harris died in the lethal gas chamber at San Quentin.

In 1993, the Legislature authorized the use of lethal injection as well as lethal gas and allowed inmates to select the method of execution to be used. The primary method of execution remained lethal gas; if the offender did not specify a preferred method of execution, lethal gas was the default method to be used. However, in October 1994, a U.S. District Judge ruled that the lethal gas chamber in California constituted cruel and unusual punishment, in violation of both state and federal constitutions, thus preventing California from using lethal gas as a method of execution. This ruling was upheld by the U.S. Ninth Circuit Court of Appeals in February, 1996.[6] The case was appealed to the U.S. Supreme Court, who remanded the case back to the Ninth Circuit for reconsideration after California modified the penal code to make lethal injection the primary method of execution in California, unless the inmate specifically requests lethal gas. The first execution by lethal injection in California was held on February 23, 1996 when William Bonin, a serial killer convicted of sexually assaulting and killing 14 boys, was put to death.

CAPITAL PUNISHMENT IN CALIFORNIA TODAY

Between 1893, when the state took over the responsibility of carrying out executions, and 2002, a total of 510 individuals have been executed in California. This number includes 506 males and four females. Of these 510 executed offenders, 307 died by hanging, 196 by lethal gas, and 7 by lethal injection.[7] The majority of those executed died between 1893 and 1967. No offenders were put to death between 1967 and 1992. Between 1992 and 2002, 10 inmates were put to death in California. In addition, one inmate who was sentenced to death in California was actually put to death in Missouri. He had dual death sentences in Missouri and California, was extradited to Missouri in 1998 and executed in that state in 1999.[8]

As of March 31, 2002, there were a total of 610 inmates under sentence of death in California. Of these, 580 men are housed in a maximum security unit at San Quentin State Prison while 12 condemned female offenders are housed in a maximum security unit at the Central California Women's Facility at Chowchilla. Six are housed in other locations, including a hospital, a mental health facility, and other state prisons. Eight are currently out to court and four are serving time in another state.[9]

Approximately 41 percent of the condemned offenders are white, 34 percent are black, 19 percent are Hispanic, and 5 percent are of other racial or ethnic backgrounds. The majority of offenders (68 percent) are between the ages of 30 and 59. Thirty percent of all condemned inmates were sentenced in Los Angeles County.[10] California state law mandates a minimum age of 18 at the time of the crime for an offender to be eligible for the death penalty. The state does allow the execution of mentally retarded offenders.[11] However, the law does not allow the execution of an insane inmate[12] or a pregnant inmate.[13] Currently both lethal gas and lethal injection are legal methods of execution, with lethal injection as the default method if the inmate does not select a method. Hanging, electrocution, and the use of the firing squad are not permitted in California.[14]

Cases of capital murder are tried in the superior court using a bifurcated trial procedure[15] that involves a jury at both the guilt and sentencing phases. An offender convicted of first degree murder is not eligible for the death penalty unless the jury at the guilt phase of the trial also determines beyond a reasonable doubt that at least one aggravating or special circumstance exists. The special circumstances that allow a sentence of death to be imposed for the crime of first degree murder includes:

> (1) The murder was intentional and carried out for financial gain.
> (2) The defendant was convicted previously of murder in the first or second degree...
> (3) The defendant, in this proceeding, has been convicted of more than one offense of murder in the first or second degree.
> (4) The murder was committed by means of a destructive device, bomb, or explosive planted, hidden, or concealed in any place, area, dwelling, building, or structure, and the defendant knew, or reasonably should have known, that his or her act or acts would create a great risk of death to one or more human beings.
> (5) The murder was committed for the purpose of avoiding or preventing a lawful arrest, or perfecting or attempting to perfect, an escape from lawful custody.
> (6) The murder was committed by means of a destructive device, bomb, or explosive that the defendant mailed or delivered, attempted to mail or deliver, or caused to be mailed or delivered, and the defendant knew, or reasonably should have known, that his or her act or acts would create a great risk of death to one or more human beings.
> (7) The victim was a peace officer ... who, while engaged in the course of the performance of his or her duties, was intentionally killed, and the defendant knew, or reasonably should have known, that the victim was a peace officer engaged in the performance of his or her duties; or the victim was a peace officer ... or a former peace officer ... and was intentionally killed in retaliation for the performance of his or her official duties.
> (8) The victim was a federal law enforcement officer or agent who, while engaged in the course of the performance of his or her duties, was intentionally killed, and the defendant knew, or reasonably should have known, that the victim was a federal law enforcement officer or agent engaged in the performance of his or her duties; or the victim was a federal law enforcement officer or agent, and was intentionally killed in retaliation for the performance of his or her official duties.
> (9) The victim was a firefighter ... who, while engaged in the course of the performance of his or her duties, was intentionally killed, and the defendant knew, or reasonably should have known, that the victim was a firefighter engaged in the performance of his or her duties.
> (10) The victim was a witness to a crime who was intentionally killed for the purpose of preventing his or her testimony in any criminal or juvenile proceeding, and the killing was not committed during the commission or attempted commission, of the crime to which he or she was a witness; or the victim was a witness to a crime and was intentionally killed in retaliation for his or her testimony in any criminal or juvenile proceeding...
> (11) The victim was a prosecutor or assistant prosecutor or a former prosecutor or assistant prosecutor of any local or state prosecutor's office in this or any other state, or of a federal prosecutor's office, and the murder was

intentionally carried out in retaliation for, or to prevent the performance of, the victim's official duties.

(12) The victim was a judge or former judge of any court of record in the local, state, or federal system in this or any other state, and the murder was intentionally carried out in retaliation for, or to prevent the performance of, the victim's official duties.

(13) The victim was an elected or appointed official or former official of the federal government, or of any local or state government of this or any other state, and the killing was intentionally carried out in retaliation for, or to prevent the performance of, the victim's official duties.

(14) The murder was especially heinous, atrocious, or cruel, manifesting exceptional depravity...

(15) The defendant intentionally killed the victim by means of lying in wait.

(16) The victim was intentionally killed because of his or her race, color, religion, nationality, or country of origin.

(17) The murder was committed while the defendant was engaged in, or was an accomplice in, the commission of, attempted commission of, or the immediate flight after committing, or attempting to commit, the following felonies:

- (A) Robbery...
- (B) Kidnapping...
- (C) Rape...
- (D) Sodomy...
- (E) The performance of a lewd or lascivious act upon the person of a child under the age of 14 years...
- (F) Oral copulation...
- (G) Burglary in the first or second degree...
- (H) Arson...
- (I) Train wrecking...
- (J) Mayhem...
- (K) Rape by instrument...
- (L) Carjacking...
- (M) To prove the special circumstances of kidnapping in subparagraph (B), or arson in subparagraph (H), if there is specific intent to kill, it is only required that there be proof of the elements of those felonies. If so established, those two special circumstances are proven even if the felony of kidnapping or arson is committed primarily or solely for the purpose of facilitating the murder.

(18) The murder was intentional and involved the infliction of torture.

(19) The defendant intentionally killed the victim by the administration of poison.

(20) The victim was a juror in any court of record in the local, state, or federal system in this or any other state, and the murder was intentionally carried out in retaliation for, or to prevent the performance of, the victim's official duties.

(21) The murder was intentional and perpetrated by means of discharging a firearm from a motor vehicle, intentionally at another person or persons outside the vehicle with the intent to inflict death...

(22) The defendant intentionally killed the victim while the defendant was an active participant in a criminal street gang ... and the murder was carried out to further the activities of the criminal street gang.[16]

If the trial jury finds that at least one of the special circumstances listed in PC §190.2(a) exists, the defendant is eligible to be sentenced to death. In most cases, the same jury is used for the sentencing phase of the trial if the prosecution is seeking the death penalty. The sentencing jury considers a number of factors when determining the penalty. These are listed in PC §190.3 and include:

> (a) The circumstances of the crime of which the defendant was convicted in the present proceeding and the existence of any special circumstances found to be true pursuant...
> (b) The presence or absence of criminal activity by the defendant which involved the use or attempted use of force or violence or the express or implied threat to use force or violence.
> (c) The presence or absence of any prior felony conviction.
> (d) Whether or not the offense was committed while the defendant was under the influence of extreme mental or emotional disturbance.
> (e) Whether or not the victim was a participant in the defendant's homicidal conduct or consented to the homicidal act.
> (f) Whether or not the offense was committed under circumstances which the defendant reasonably believed to be a moral justification or extenuation for his conduct.
> (g) Whether or not defendant acted under extreme duress or under the substantial domination of another person.
> (h) Whether or not at the time of the offense the capacity of the defendant to appreciate the criminality of his conduct or to conform his conduct to the requirements of law was impaired as a result of mental disease or defect, or the affects of intoxication.
> (i) The age of the defendant at the time of the crime.
> (j) Whether or not the defendant was an accomplice to the offense and his participation in the commission of the offense was relatively minor.
> (k) Any other circumstance which extenuates the gravity of the crime even though it is not a legal excuse for the crime.

Many of these, especially the last, are factors in mitigation. After considering these factors, the jury may only return a sentence of death if it finds that the aggravating factors substantially outweigh the mitigating factors.[17] In all other situations, the sentencing jury must impose a sentence of life imprisonment without the possibility of parole.

All cases in which a sentence of death has been handed down must be automatically reviewed by the California State Supreme Court. A defendant may not waive his/her right to this review as it is mandated by statute. The Court has three options when hearing death penalty cases; it may:

- affirm the conviction and the sentence of death
- affirm the conviction but reverse the death sentence, which will result in a retrial of the sentencing phase only
- reverse the conviction, which will result in a new trial

If the Court does affirm the sentence of death, the inmate has the option of filing a writ of *habeas corpus*, which requires the court to review the legality of the inmate's imprisonment. *Habeas corpus* claims generally concern issues of whether the defendant received a fair trial. Because they frequently include issues which may not be reflected in the trial court records, they may require independent investigation. Examples of *habeas corpus* include claims that the defendant's appointed counsel provided ineffective assistance and claims that the district attorney failed to disclose certain evidence. A writ of *habeas corpus* may be heard in both state and federal courts. Generally, a new attorney is appointed by the federal courts for a federal *habeas corpus* claim.

The majority of inmates on death row are indigent and cannot afford an attorney when making appeals. In 1976, the **Office of the State Public Defender** (OSPD) was created by the Legislature. Its original purpose was to provide legal representation for indigent criminal defendants who had been convicted of both capital and non-capital felonies and who were appealing their convictions to a higher court. However, because of the increasing number of condemned offenders requiring counsel, the mandate of the OSPD was changed in 1990 to focus exclusively on capital cases in the California Supreme Court and in the U.S. Supreme Court.[18]

THE COST OF EXECUTIONS IN CALIFORNIA TODAY

It is difficult to determine the actual total cost of carrying out an execution in California. The average cost of housing an inmate is approximately $26,894 per year. Department of Corrections staff who are assigned to an execution team receive their regular salaries, which are budgeted by the state. The cost of the actual execution procedure, including the chemicals used for the lethal injection, is minimal.[19]

However, the real cost involved in capital punishment, which makes it more expensive than a sentence of life imprisonment without parole, comes from the appellate court reviews. There are a number of constitutionally mandated safeguards which protect offenders. These include:

- Juries must be provided with clear sentencing guidelines that clearly explain what constitutes both aggravating and mitigating circumstances.

- Defendants must have a dual or bifurcated trial. The first segment of the trial establishes the defendant's guilt or innocence on the capital charge and, if the defendant is found guilty, whether or not he/she is eligible for the death penalty. The second phase determines whether the defendant will be sentenced to death or to life imprisonment without the possibility of parole.

- All cases involving a sentence of death are automatically appealed to the California Supreme Court. The offender may not waive his/her right to appeal and the Supreme Court is required to hear all capital appeals.

- Indigent defendants under a sentence of death are entitled to counsel which is provided, and paid for, by the state.

These constitutional safeguards significantly increase the costs of a capital sentence. The jury selection process for a capital case often is much more extensive than in non-capital crimes. Because the trial process is bifurcated, it is longer and more expensive. Capital trials frequently involve the use of more investigators and more expert testimony in court, which increases the costs to both the prosecution and the defense. Finally, the automatic mandatory appeal to the Supreme Court creates an additional expense for the state. Because very few defendants are willing to plead guilty to a capital charge, almost every trial conducted for a capital crime requires a jury trial and incurs all these requirements and expenses.

THE EXECUTION PROCEDURE IN CALIFORNIA

Death Row

PC §3603 states that "The judgment of death shall be executed within the walls of the California State Prison at San Quentin." Until recently, all male prisoners under sentence of death were housed in a maximum security unit at San Quentin. However, in 2001, PC §3600 was modified to create certain exceptions. A condemned inmate who commits one of a specified list of serious violent offenses or who orders other members of a prison gang to commit these offenses may be housed in a secure condemned unit at the California State Prison, Sacramento. Condemned inmates who have serious medical or mental conditions that may endanger the inmate or others may be housed at the California Medical Facility or some other appropriate institution. Female condemned prisoners are housed in a maximum security unit at the Central California Women's Facility at Chowchilla.[20] Female offenders, and male offenders not housed at San Quentin, are moved to San Quentin for the actual execution procedure.

The Execution Chamber

All executions are held in the California execution chamber, a self-contained unit housed at San Quentin. The unit includes six separate areas:

1. The **execution chamber** – a small octagonal chamber approximately 7.5 feet in diameter with a large oval door at the rear
2. A **witness area** with a window view of the execution chamber
3. An **anteroom** from which the lethal injection is administered and which contains three telephones, one of which is kept open for the Governor's use, one of which is for the use of the California Supreme Court and the Attorney General's Office, and one of which is connected to the Warden's office. The valves and levers used for executions by lethal gas are also found in this room
4. A **chemical room** which includes storage cabinets and a work bench, as well as the chemical mixing pots, pipes, and valves that are used for lethal gas executions
5. Two **holding cells**, each containing a toilet and room for a mattress
6. An **officer's area** which includes a kitchen and resting area for the staff[20]

A maximum of 50 people may witness an execution. PC §3605 states that the warden of San Quentin must be present at the execution and must invite the Attorney General, twelve reputable citizens, up to five family members or friends of the inmate (if requested), and up to two spiritual advisors of the inmate (if requested). No one under the age of 18 may witness an execution. The witnesses observe the execution from the witness area of the execution chamber while the warden generally sits in the anteroom. In addition, California state procedures also allow for up to 17 representatives of the news media, nine state-selected witnesses, and four staff escorts.

The Procedure for Lethal Injection in California

When the actual execution order is received, the condemned inmate is moved into a special security area of death row. They receive priority visiting privileges and are checked hourly by staff. Two pre-execution reports are prepared. The first report is completed 20 days prior to the execution and includes the following information:

- a psychiatric report to determine the inmate's sanity
- a report from the chaplain
- a summary of the inmate's behavior, including observations by custody staff and the offender's case worker
- a cover letter from the prison warden which includes information obtained from interviews or other communications with the inmate and the inmate's family and/or friends

The second report is prepared seven days prior to the execution and, in addition to the above information, also includes a review of any changes that may have occurred since the completion of the first report.[21]

The California Department of Corrections website includes a description of the condemned inmate's last 24 hours before an execution by lethal injection:

> During the day before the execution, the warden will make special arrangements for visits by approved family members, spiritual advisors, and friends.
>
> About 6 p.m. the day before the execution, the inmate will be moved to the death watch cell which is adjacent to the execution chamber. From then on, a three-member staff unit will provide a constant death watch.
>
> Soon after he is rehoused, the inmate will be served his last dinner meal. The prison makes every effort to provide the meal requested by the inmate.
>
> Between 7 and 10 p.m., the inmate may be visited by the assigned state chaplain and the warden. The inmate may read, watch television, or play the radio. He can request special food items and coffee or soft drinks.
>
> The family, spiritual advisors and friends the inmate has selected as witnesses may arrive up to two hours before the scheduled execution.
>
> About 30 minutes before the scheduled execution, the inmate is given a new pair of denim trousers and blue work shirt to wear. He is escorted into the execution chamber a few minutes before the appointed time and is strapped onto a table. [The chairs previously used for lethal gas executions have been removed.]

> The inmate is connected to a cardiac monitor which is connected to a printer outside the execution chamber. An IV is started in two usable veins and a flow of normal saline solution is administered at a slow rate. [One line is held in reserve in case of a blockage or malfunction in the other.] The door is closed. The warden issues the execution order.[22]

The execution involves injections of three separate chemicals, each of which is lethal in the amounts administered to the offender. These include:

- 5.0 grams of sodium pentothal in 20-25 cc of diluent
- 50 cc of pancuronium bromide
- 50 cc of potassium chloride

The actual execution procedure is described on the California Department of Corrections website:

> At the warden's signal, sodium pentothal is administered, then the line is flushed with sterile normal saline solution. This is followed by pancuronium bromide, a saline flush, and finally, potassium chloride. As required by the California Penal Code, a physician is present to declare when death occurs.
>
> After all witnesses have left, the body is removed with dignity and care. Typically, the family claims the body. If not, the State makes the arrangements.[23]

NOTES

1. Information in this section obtained from the California Department of Corrections: Capital Punishment (http://www.cdc.state.ca.us/communicationsoffice/capitalpunishment)
2. *People v. Anderson*, 6 Cal. 3d 628, 493 P.2d 880, 100 Cal. Rptr. 152, cert. denied, 406 U.S. 958 (1972)
3. *Furman v. Georgia*, 408 U.S. 238 (1972)
4. *Gregg v. Georgia*, 428 U.S. 153 (1976)
5. *Rockwell v. Superior Court*, 18 Cal. 3d 420, 556 P.2d 1101, 134 Cal. Rptr. 650 (1976).
6. *Fierro v. Gomez*, 77 F. 3d 301 (1996)
7. California Department of Corrections: Capital Punishment
8. *Ibid*
9. *Ibid*
10. *Ibid*
11. Death Penalty Information Center: California (http://www.deathpenaltyinfo.org/california.html)
12. PC §3700 to PC §3704
13. PC §3706
14. PC §3604
15. PC §190.1
16. PC §190.2(a)
17. *People v. Tuilaepa*, 4 Cal. 4th 569, 842 P.2d 1142, 15 Cal. Rptr. 2d 382 (1992)
18. Office of the State Public Defender home page (http://www.ospd.ca.gov/)

19. California Department of Corrections: Capital Punishment
20. PC §3601
21. California Department of Corrections: Capital Punishment
22. *Ibid*
23. *Ibid*

CHAPTER 8

CORRECTIONS IN CALIFORNIA

INTRODUCTION

California's correctional program is based in the **Youth and Adult Correctional Agency** (YACA), which is chaired by a state cabinet-level secretary. The mission of the YACA is

> to develop and implement effective and innovative correctional policy, create a coordinated correctional system which is responsive to the citizen's right to public safety and governmental accountability, and maintain a reputation for excellence and integrity.[1]

Essentially, the YACA is responsible for overseeing a variety of departments and boards, ensuring that the state correctional system runs in an efficient and organized manner, and maintaining standardized correctional policy throughout the system. The departments that the YACA oversees include:

- The California Department of Corrections
- The Board of Prison Terms
- The Board of Corrections
- The California Youth Authority
- The Youthful Offender Parole Board
- The Prison Industry Authority

JAILS IN CALIFORNIA

In California the primary difference between a **jail** and a **prison** is that prisons are usually run by the state whereas jails are managed by the county or local municipality. Inmates of state prison facilities are offenders who have been convicted of a felony offense and who have been sentenced to serve a term of incarceration of at least one year. Inmates in county jails may be convicted offenders serving sentences of less than one year or may be defendants who are incarcerated while awaiting trial or sentencing. The average length of stay in a jail is much shorter than in a prison; some inmates may only stay a few hours whereas others may be held for several years while awaiting trial.

County jails in California have four main functions. These are enumerated in PC §4000:

> (a) For the detention of persons committed in order to secure their attendance as witnesses in criminal cases;
> (b) For the detention of persons charged with crime and committed for trial;

(c) For the confinement of persons committed for contempt, or upon civil process, or by other authority of law;
(d) For the confinement of persons sentenced to imprisonment therein upon a conviction for crime.

Jails or local detention facilities in California are divided into four main types. A Type I facility is defined as:

> "a local detention facility used for the detention of persons for not more than 96 hours excluding holidays after booking. Such a Type I facility may also detain persons on court order either for their own safekeeping or sentenced to a city jail as an inmate worker, and may house inmate workers sentenced to the county jail provided such placement in the facility is made on a voluntary basis on the part of the inmate.[2]

A Type II facility is "used for the detention of persons pending arraignment, during trial, and upon a sentence of commitment."[3] A Type III facility is "used only for the detention of convicted and sentenced persons."[4] Finally, a Type IV facility is "a local detention facility or portion thereof designated for the housing of inmates eligible ... for work/education furlough and/or other programs involving inmate access into the community."[5] Essentially, Type I facilities are short-term holding cells for arrested offenders who are moved to a Type II facility within the specified period of time.

California has 57 county jail systems, which are operated primarily by sheriffs.[6] Alpine County has no jails. Most county jail systems are locally funded and independently operated, although they are required to comply with state-wide standards for the construction and operation of jail facilities and for staff training. The county jails share the responsibility for administering sanctions to convicted offenders with the state prison system.

Jails in California are overseen by the **California Board of Corrections** (BOC). The BOC was originally established in 1944 and is under the aegis of the YACA.[7] According to PC §6025(a), the BOC contains a total of 15 members, twelve of whom are appointed by the governor with the advice and consent of the YACA and the Senate. Two of these are members of the general public while the rest are representatives of specific elements and agencies of local adult and juvenile criminal justice systems. The other three members of the BOC are required by statute: the Secretary of YACA (who chairs the BOC), the Director of Corrections, and the Director of the Youth Authority.

According to the BOC website, the agency has a number of responsibilities:

> The Board of Corrections (BOC) works in partnership with city and county officials to develop and maintain standards for the construction and operation of local jails and juvenile detention facilities, and for the employment and training of local corrections and probation personnel. The BOC also inspects local adult and juvenile detention facilities; disburses training funds; administers grant programs that respond to facility construction needs, juvenile crime and delinquency, and mentally ill offenders; and conducts special studies relative to the public safety of California's communities.[8]

The Los Angeles County Jail System

The **Los Angeles County Sheriff's Department** (LASD) operates the largest jail system in the world. The **Custody Operations Division** is responsible for the operation of the eight custodial facilities while the **Correctional Services Division** operates a variety of auxiliary units that provide service to the jails.

The **Twin Towers Correctional Facility**, which opened in 1997, is the largest jail facility in the world. Twin Towers has a staff of over 2,400, including both sworn personnel and civilians, and includes a maximum security Type II jail, an inmate reception center, and a custodial medical treatment center. The facility houses almost 4,200 inmates. Each tower uses the Panopticon design originated by Jeremy Bentham.[9]

The **North County Correctional Facility** uses a campus design with five housing pods. In 2002, the average daily inmate population of this facility was 3,675. North County offers inmates the opportunity to participate in one of three vocational training programs: sign production, clothing manufacture, and printing. These programs not only provide offenders with vocational training but also substantially offset the cost of operating the facility. In addition, the facility's Amer-I-Can Program is a 60-hour program that teaches "life management" skills, focusing on developing positive self-esteem and self-determination.[10] The Department's **South Facility**, located on the Peter J. Pitchess Detention Center (PDC) in Saugus, offers vocational programs in carpentry, masonry, welding, and dog grooming. Inmates may also receive fire service training and work with the County Fire Department as fire suppression crews.[11]

The **Mira Loma Detention Facility** is built on the site of a former Air Force training field. It was originally opened in 1954 as a jail for inmates with tuberculosis. The facility was closed in 1979 but in 1983, the department re-opened it in response to a problem of jail overcrowding. In 1986, the facility began to house female as well as male inmates. In 1993, the county again closed Mira Loma. In 1997, the LASD and the U.S. Immigration and Naturalization Service joined forces and re-opened Mira Loma as a facility to house medium security federal detainees who are awaiting deportation hearings. The facility provides detainees with medical, religious, and educational programs, and deportation hearings are conducted on the site of the facility.[12]

PRISONS IN CALIFORNIA

History of the California Department of Corrections

The California state prison system was created during the period of the California gold rush and evolved and grew over time. In 1851, the California State Legislature authorized the lease of 83 state prisoners, including one woman, to two private contractors, General M.G. Vallejo and J.M. Estell, although Vallejo later sold his interest in the contract to Estell, who became the sole lessee of the inmates. Estell used inmate labor to build the first state prison, San Quentin. During the day, the inmates worked to build the prison while at night they were locked on board a prison ship, the *Waban*. The first cell block of the prison, known as the "Stone Building," was completed in 1854. It had no plumbing, heat, or lighting. During its first year of operation a total of 83 inmates escaped from San Quentin. Eight years later, in 1862, a mass escape occurred in which 300 inmates broke out of the prison.

In 1858, the state Legislature authorized the construction of a second state prison at Folsom, although work did not actually begin until 1874. Folsom Prison was completed in 1880, and the first 44 inmates were transferred from San Quentin. In 1891, the inmates constructed a dam, powerhouse, and canal to generate hydroelectric power. The powerhouse was eventually converted to vocational classrooms that are still in use today.

Reports of corruption and brutality on the part of the private contractors running the prisons forced the state to take permanent control of the prison system in 1861. A non-salaried, three-man Board of Prison Directors provided a small amount of control but most policy decisions were made by individual prison wardens, who were constantly changing due to political upheavals at the state level. This lack of managerial continuity led to frequent changes in prison management and policy.

Some of the key events of the late 1800s and early 1900s that affected the California prison system included:

- 1864 – the passage of the state's first "good time" law, which allowed prison wardens to give inmates up to five days off their sentences for each month of work and good behavior
- 1879 – the passage of the convict labor law, which prohibited the use of convict labor that competed with private enterprise
- 1893 – the passage of the parole law. The warden of San Quentin State Prison served as the state's first parole officer
- 1893 – the first state execution took place at San Quentin on March 3rd
- 1895 – the first execution held at Folsom State Prison on December 13th
- 1903 – the escape of 15 inmates from Folsom State Prison. inmates took 12 hostages, including the warden. The inmates gained access to the prison armory, leading to the death of one correctional officer and the serious injury of another. This event may have contributed to California's non-hostage policy: in California, no inmate will be freed in exchange for a hostage

During this period, the majority of women inmates were housed at San Quentin, although a few were held at Folsom between 1885 and 1929. Female inmates in San Quentin were originally housed together in a single room and were later moved to the basement of the prison. Between 1922 and 1923, San Quentin sent a small number of women who had been convicted of vice crimes to the State Industrial Farm for Women at Sonoma. In 1924, responding to pressure from women's groups, the Legislature authorized the construction of a separate building for women at San Quentin. In 1929, the Legislature authorized the construction of a separate women's prison at Tehachapi. The building was completed in 1932. In 1936, a separate Board of Trustees for the new prison took over responsibility for the state's female inmates.

In 1937, the State Legislature replaced hanging with lethal gas as the official form of execution. A gas chamber was constructed and installed at San Quentin. It was first used on

December 2, 1938. The last execution by hanging conducted at Folsom Prison occurred on December 3, 1937; the last hanging at San Quentin was conducted on May 1, 1942.

In 1941, the California Institution for Men at Chino was opened. As a "prison without walls", it housed mild, first-time offenders and, by separating them from serious, hardened criminals, was a notable experiment in reform and rehabilitation. The prison was expanded in 1953, although walls and fences were constructed in 1983 after an inmate escaped from the institution and murdered three Chino residents.

In 1944, then-governor of California, Earl Warren, created the California Department of Corrections (CDC). The CDC centralized the management and operation of all state prisons under a new Director of Corrections. The first Director, Richard A. McGee, developed and refined the medical model of prison management.

During the next ten years, the CDC continued to open new correctional facilities. In 1946, the Deuel Vocational Institution (DVI) was opened on an abandoned army base near Lancaster. It was moved to Tracy in 1953. DVI housed 500 young offenders who were considered too young for prison but not suitable for other youth facilities. The Correctional Training Facility at Soledad also opened in 1946. In 1950, the California Medical Facility began providing treatment for mentally impaired or chronically ill inmates. The California Institute for Women opened in 1952 near Corono after an earthquake seriously damaged the prison at Tehachapi and the California Men's Colony opened in San Luis Obispo in 1954. In 1953, the California Youth Authority (CYA) was formally established. In addition, in 1947, Correctional Industries began operations. The program was designed to work with private industry and labor and to employ inmates. It was renamed the Prison Industry Authority in 1983.

During the 1950s, the CDC increasingly emphasized rehabilitation and by 1960 over 10,000 inmates were enrolled in some type of group counseling. However, by the late 1960s, most of these programs were phased out due to a lack of evidence that such counseling had any significant positive effect on the inmates. In 1957, the CDC took over the responsibility for supervising adult males on parole. The concept of "differentiated supervision" was developed, which bases the level of parole supervision on the parolee's potential risk to public safety.

In 1961, the state Legislature created the Youth and Adult Correctional Agency (YACA) to oversee all aspects of the California state correctional system. The first administrator of YACA, Richard McGee, was formerly the director of the CDC.

The advent of prison gangs in the late 1960s and early 1970s led to an increase in prison violence. Between 1970 and 1974, 116 inmates were killed and 11 employees were killed by inmates. At the same time, the inmate population was actually decreasing: between 1964 and 1974, the inmate population dropped by nearly 2000. In 1971, the commitment rate dropped to an all-time low: only 9.7 percent of convicted felons were sent to state prison in that year.

In 1966, a statewide affirmative action program led to an increase in the number of women and minorities employed in the Department of Corrections. In 1967, the first male correctional officer was assigned to work in a women's facility and in 1971, the first woman correctional officer position was established and the first woman was assigned to work in a male prison. This significantly increased women's opportunities for promotion and job development within the CDC. The first female warden of a male correctional institution was appointed in 1982.

In 1972, the CDC established the first Correctional Training Center to train new correctional officers. By 1983, the program had developed into a six-week long training academy.

In 1975, the Legislature enacted the Inmate Bill of Rights. Rights provided to the inmates included the right to have conjugal visits, to own property, to marry while in prison, and to receive published materials. However, in 1994, the Bill of Rights was extensively modified, with many of the rights outlined in the 1975 law being eliminated or at least severely limited.

In the late 1970s, the state's sentencing structure was significantly revised and updated. The passage of the Determinate Sentencing Law in 1976 made punishment the official purpose of incarceration and set a specific prison term for almost every offense in the California Penal Code. Only those offenders convicted of first or second degree murder continued to receive indeterminate sentences and parole hearings.

By the end of 1977, the inmate population had dropped to its lowest point since the late 1950s. However, in the late 1970s and early 1980s, the number of incarcerated offenders increased significantly and the CDC began to develop plans for a large-scale prison construction program. In 1980, California had twelve state prisons; by 1990, there were 29. The increase in the prison population continued due to get-tough statutes such as the 1994 "Three- Strikes Law." One of the most well-known prisons to open during this period was Pelican Bay State Prison, which opened in 1989. A maximum security prison, Pelican Bay includes California's first high-tech security housing unit, the most secure prison facility in the state. When Pelican Bay was first opened, CDC transferred approximately 1600 of the most disruptive and violent inmates in the state to the facility. Inmate violence statewide showed an immediate and significant drop. In 1990, the Central California Women's Facility near Chowchilla was opened. It is believed to be the largest women's prison in the world and currently houses over 3,100 inmates.

Prison management has also become more complex as the prison service had to deal with issues such as AIDS and tuberculosis. The number of HIV-positive inmates in the state prison system has increased significantly in the past decades. The CDC also began to focus on issues relating to crime victims. In 1988, the CDC created the Victim Services Program to help victims understand and exercise their rights within the correctional system and to help offenders understand the effect crime has on victims.

Today, the CDC is the largest single department in the California state government. The 2002-2003 Budget Act gave the CDC a budget of $5.2 billion, approximately 6 percent of the state General Fund. The CDC currently employs 49,052 people, including 41,856 in various correctional institutions, 3,074 in parole, and 4,122 in administration. Over 30,000 of these are sworn peace officers.[13]

The CDC and Prisons Today

The CDC operates all state prisons as well as various community-based correctional facilities throughout the state and is responsible for supervising all parolees. The CDC operates a total of 33 state prisons, at all custody levels. Pelican Bay is the most secure facility in the state. The CDC also operates 38 minimum-security prison camps (three of which house female inmates), which train inmates in fire-suppression techniques, 16 community correctional facilities, and five Prisoner Mother/Infant Programs. In 2002, there were 159,695 felons currently housed in these facilities. Los Angeles accounted for approximately 33.5 percent of the inmate population, followed by San Diego, which accounted for 7.5 percent, and San Bernardino, with 6.6 percent. The average yearly cost to maintain an offender in 2002 was $28,502. Nearly 50 percent of this cost is attributed to maintaining security in the various institutions.

Approximately 94 percent of all inmates housed by the CDC in 2002 were male and 6 percent were female. Approximately 29 percent were white, 30 percent black, 35 percent Hispanic, and 5.5 percent were classified as some other racial or ethnic group. The average age was 35 and the average reading level of an inmate was seventh grade. Almost 48 percent of the inmates were convicted of violent crimes against persons, 21 percent were convicted of property crimes, 24 percent of drug-related offenses, and 7.5 percent of other felony offenses. The average sentence for a felony offender in California was 41.4 months and the average time served was 25.1 months.[14]

The California Prison Industry Authority

The **Prison Industry Authority** (PIA) was authorized by PC §2800. According to PC §2801, the PIA has three main purposes:

> (a) To develop and operate industrial, agricultural, and service enterprises employing prisoners in institutions under the jurisdiction of the Department of Corrections, which enterprises may be located either within those institutions or elsewhere...
> (b) To create and maintain working conditions within the enterprises as much like those which prevail in private industry as possible, to assure prisoners employed therein the opportunity to work productively, to earn funds, and to acquire or improve effective work habits and occupational skills.
> (c) To operate a work program for prisoners which will ultimately be self-supporting by generating sufficient funds from the sale of products and services to pay all the expenses of the program, and one which will provide goods and services which are or will be used by the Department of Corrections, thereby reducing the cost of its operation.

Essentially, PIA provides job opportunities for inmates who are incarcerated in various California state correctional institutions. Participation in PIA is voluntary but many inmates want to work and many PIA work assignments have waiting lists. Over 6,500 inmates are employed through PIA in over 65 different industries. Products produced by PIA programs and services provided by inmates in PIA programs are available to local, state, and federal government agencies. Inmates employed in PIA programs receive salaries ranging from $0.30 to $0.95. Up to 20 percent of an inmate's wages can be deducted for fines and court-ordered restitution.

Products for sale through PIA include office furniture, food equipment, food products (including milk, meat and chicken products, and coffee), bedding, clothing, boots and shoes, cleaning products, indoor and outdoor flags, signs and decals, and various textile products. Services available from PIA include printing, laundry, dental, and digital services.[15]

The Joint Venture Program

Like the PIA, the CDC's **Joint Venture Program** (JVP) also provides prison inmates with opportunities to work while incarcerated. The program was established by Proposition 193, passed by California voters in 1990. The Proposition allows private businesses to contract with the CDC to set up business operations inside prisons and to hire inmates to work in these programs. Inmates produce a variety of goods and services for sale. They are paid wages similar to those received by non-inmates for similar work. Inmate wages are subject to deductions for taxes, room and board, victim compensation costs, and support for the inmate's family. The inmate may also be required to save a certain portion of his or her wages for release.

As of 2003, over 30 prisons in the state had operating JVPs. According to the CDC, the program has a number of benefits for participating employers, including:

- the state offers tax incentives to employers participating in JVPs
- employers do not need to provide benefits such as retirement, sick leave, vacation leave, medical insurance, etc.
- employers may qualify for discounted rates on workers' compensation insurance
- employers have an on-call labor pool

The economic benefits include:

- employed offenders receiving a living wage pay restitution to crime victims
- employed inmates pay taxes to the state
- room and board are deducted from the inmates' wages, reducing or fully defraying the cost of incarceration
- family support is deducted from the inmates' wages, reducing the cost to social welfare programs
- inmates are required to participate in a mandatory savings program for release, which helps them adjust when released on parole.[16]

PAROLE IN CALIFORNIA

Parole is not a sentence. It is actually a form of early release from a sentence of incarceration. In California, parole hearings are held by the California Board of Prison Terms. Once the offender is released from incarceration, he or she is supervised by the California Department of Corrections' Parole and Community Services Division.

The California Board of Prison Terms

The **California Board of Prison Terms** (BPT) was founded in 1944. It serves as California's adult parole board, conducting parole hearings for all inmates whose sentences include the possibility of parole. The BPT also sets the terms and conditions for all offenders released on parole and conducts revocation hearings for offenders who violate those terms and conditions. The BPT also conducts certification, placement, and revocation hearings for mentally disordered offenders as well as probable cause hearings for violent sexual offenders whose parole status has been revoked.

At the request of the state governor, the BPT may also consider applications reprieves, pardons, and commutations of sentences. The Board will investigate these applications and make recommendations to the governor. The Board may also review and approve applications from California prisoners who are not U.S. citizens and who wish to be transferred to their home countries to serve out the remainder of their sentences. The BPT reviews a variety of requests from offenders, including requests for reconsideration of denial of good-time credit and requests to modify the length or conditions of parole.[17]

The BPT consists of nine full-time commissioners who are appointed by the governor with the advice and consent of the senate. Members serve staggered terms of four years and are eligible to be reappointed. The governor designates the chair of the BPT, who acts as the Board's administrative head.[18] In addition to the nine commissioners, there are approximately 60 deputy commissioners located throughout the state. Parole hearings are conducted at institutions throughout the state by a panel of three individuals, including two commissioners and one deputy commissioner.[19]

The BPT only becomes involved when an offender has received an indeterminate sentence, a sentence for which there is no fixed term of imprisonment. The most common such sentence is the term of life in prison with the possibility of parole. In California, offenders sentenced to an indeterminate sentence are required to serve a minimum term before they become eligible to go before the BPT for a parole consideration hearing. These offenders will not be granted parole unless the BPT decides that they are suitable for release and do not pose an unreasonable risk of danger to the public. However, if the governor grants a pardon or compassionate release, the BPT is not required to make such a determination of suitability.

Offenders who have determinate, or fixed, sentences must be released from prison and placed on parole once they have served the terms imposed by the sentencing court. The BPT is not involved in this process.

Parole Conditions in California

All parolees are subject to a set of general conditions which they must observe. Failure to observe these conditions may lead to parole revocation. The general conditions of parole in California include:

- Parolees must report to their parole agent immediately after release from custody

- Parolees must notify their parole agent of their residence and must inform them in advance of any change of residence
- Parolees must notify their parole agent within 72 hours of any change of employer, employment location, or employment termination
- Parolees must comply with all instructions of their parole agent
- Parolees may not travel more than 50 miles from their place of residence without prior permission from the parole agent
- Parolees may not leave their county of residence for more than 48 hours
- Parolees may not leave California without prior written permission from their parole agent
- Parolees may not engage in any criminal conduct and must inform their parole agent if they are arrested for a felony or misdemeanor, cited, or released on their own recognizance for any crime
- Parolees may not own, use, or have access to any weapon
- Parolees must sign the condition of parole
- Parolees must observe any special conditions imposed by the BPT[20]

When an inmate is paroled (regardless of whether the original sentence was determinate or indeterminate), the Board has the option of imposing various special conditions of parole, in addition to the above general conditions which must be observed by every parolee. As with general conditions of parole, failure to observe any special conditions may result in the revocation of parole. Special conditions which may be imposed include:

- Participation in a psychiatric treatment program approved by the Parole and Community Services Division of the California Department of Corrections
- Total abstinence from alcoholic beverages
- Participation in anti-narcotic testing (if there is a history of drug abuse)
- Maintenance of a residence with a location approved by the Parole and Community Services Division
- No gang participation – the parolee may be ordered to not actively participate in, associate with, promote, or assist in any prison or criminal street gang activity, or wear any gang signs or paraphernalia.

Parole Supervision

All parolees released from confinement are supervised by the **Parole and Community Services Division** of the CDC. The Division oversees 32 re-entry centers, one restitution center, and one drug treatment facility. Most of these facilities are contracted out to and operated by public or private agencies and are monitored by Division staff on a regular basis. The CDC has 182 parole offices in 81 locations throughout the state, as well as 4 outpatient clinics for parolees. These facilities supervised a total of 117,183 parolees in 2002. Los Angeles accounted for over 30 percent of the parole population, followed by San Diego, which accounted for almost 7 percent. The average annual cost per parolee was $2,882 in 2002.

In 2002, males made up 89 percent of all parolees in California. Approximately 30 percent were white, 26 percent black, 38 percent Hispanic, and 5 percent from other racial or ethnic groups.

Almost 25 percent of parolees in 2002 were originally convicted of crimes against persons, 26 percent were convicted of property crimes, 40 percent of drug-related offenses, and 10 percent of other crimes. The median age of offenders on parole in 2002 was 36 years. The return rate with a new prison term was 10.6 per 100 average daily population and the return rate as a parole violator was 54.2 per 100 average population.[21]

PROBATION IN CALIFORNIA

Unlike parole, **probation** is a sentence imposed by the court. It is a form of community corrections because the sentence is served in the community rather than in a correctional institution. The offender is supervised by the court while on probation and is required to abide by various statutory and court-ordered conditions.

Although many states combine probation and parole services into one state-wide agency, California probation services are provided at the county level. Each of the 58 counties in California has a separate probation department, run by a **Chief Probation Officer**. The one exception to this is San Francisco which has both a Juvenile Probation Chief and an Adult Probation Chief. The probation department is responsible for preparing pre-sentencing reports for the court and for supervising all criminal defendants placed on probation by the court.

Through the preparation of the pre-sentence report, the probation department assists the sentencing judge by helping to identify offenders who may be suitable candidates for probation as well as those who are poor risks. In addition, the department may recommend appropriate sanctions for offenders, including custodial sentences, community service, fines, and restitution. When an offender is sentenced to a term of probation, the probation officer assigned to that offender develops a supervision plan that is based on the offender's individual needs and that is designed to help the offender work towards becoming a law-abiding citizen.

Los Angeles County Probation Department

The **Los Angeles County Probation Department** is the largest probation department in the world. It was established in 1903, when the state enacted its first probation laws. The Department has an annual budget of over $480 million and employs over 5,000 individuals.

The Department's Adult Field Services Bureau has 13 field offices and has approximately 47,000 adult probationers under supervision. The Bureau also conducts approximately 49,000 investigations annually. The Adult Special Services Bureau supervises approximately 31,000 adults in special programs, including high-risk offenders and offenders who are required to undergo regular or random narcotics testing. This Bureau conducts approximately 23,000 investigations each year as well as approximately 160,000 pretrial investigations.[22]

The San Francisco Probation Department

The San Francisco County Probation Department is unusual in that it has two Chief Probation Officers: one for the Juvenile Probation Department and one for the Adult Probation Department.

Both departments work out of the Office of the District Attorney of the City and County of San Francisco and have similar responsibilities. The adult department will be discussed here; see Chapter 9 for a discussion of juvenile probation.

The Adult Probation Department is responsible for the protection, safety, and rehabilitation of adult probationers. They are also responsible for protecting the public. The Department prepares pre-sentence investigations and reports for superior courts in San Francisco, recommends suitable sanctions for offenders, and supervises offenders while they are serving their sentence in the community. In addition, if the sentence includes victim restitution, the adult probation department is responsible for the collection of restitution payments. The department enforces all court-ordered conditions of probation and returns offenders to court if they fail to comply with these conditions or if they commit new crimes while on probation. The department also provides referrals for employers, treatment centers, and other resources.[23]

In 2002, the annual cost for supervising an adult on probation in San Francisco was approximately $890. To keep the same offender incarcerated for one year in 2002 cost approximately $25,000.[24]

VICTIMS' RIGHTS

According to PC §679.02, victims and witnesses of crime (or their next of kin) have the right, upon request, to be notified of an offender's death, release on parole, release due to the expiration of the sentence, escape, or placement in a re-entry facility.

If an offender is being considered for parole, the BPT may place special conditions on the offender, in addition to the general conditions required of all parolees. Victims are also entitled to have input into some of these special conditions of parole. For example, if the victim was clearly threatened by the offender, the victim may request that the parolee be required to live in another county, or in another city within the county. The victim may request that restrictions be placed on the offender's contact with the victim, so that if the parolee contacts the victim without prior approval from the parole officer, parole may be revoked and the offender returned to custody.[25]

BECOMING A CORRECTIONAL OFFICER

In California, correctional officers are peace officers who serve with the CDC in civil service positions. They are responsible for the protection of inmates and staff within and outside correctional institutions, as well as for the protection of the public as a whole.

The minimum standards required to apply for a position as a correctional officer in California are:

- Be at least 21 years of age at the time of appointment
- Be a U.S. citizen or a permanent resident alien who is eligible for and has applied for U.S. citizenship

- Have no felony convictions
- Be a high school graduate or equivalent (G.E.D.) or have a higher level academic degree
- Have vision of at least 20/60 in each eye, correctable to 20/20
- No color blindness
- Hearing adequate to perform the essential functions of the job
- Good physical, mental, and emotional health
- Have a history of law abiding behavior
- Be legally eligible to own and possess a firearm[25]

Individuals selected to become correctional officers go through the Basic Correctional Officer Academy training program. The academy training is a full-time program lasting for 16 weeks and including a total of 640 hours of training. Subjects included in the training include weapons training, techniques of arrest and control, law (including arrest law, constitutional law, laws of evidence), inmates' rights, search procedures, gangs, victims of crime, use of force, and disciplinary and restraint procedures.[26]

After completing academy training, officers must go through a 24-month apprenticeship program that includes at least 3,600 hours spent performing duties that are directly related to their work classification. Time spent at the academy, or in any additional training programs, may not be included in this 3,600 hours of apprenticeship. All correctional officers also receive monthly in-service training.[27]

After completing academy training, the salary range for full-time correctional officers is $2,809 to $4,573 per month. There are some additional allotments available to officers accepting assignments at certain designated institutions (e.g., Soledad, San Quentin, Avenal, Ironwood, and Calipatria State Prisons). Correctional officers also receive a $530 uniform replacement allowance. Officers who are state-certified as bilingual and recognized by the CDC as using their skills on the job receive a $100 pay differential per month.[28]

NOTES

1. California Youth and Adult Correctional Agency home page (http://www.yaca.state.ca.us/)
2. California Board of Corrections (2002). *Jail Profile Survey: Annual Report 2001* Available online at http://www.bdcorr.ca.gov/index.htm
3. *Ibid*
4. *Ibid*
5. *Ibid*
6. *Ibid*
7. PC §6024
8. California Board of Corrections home page (http://www.bdcorr.ca.gov)
9. Los Angeles Sheriff's Department Custody Operations Division web page (http://www.lasd.org/custody/index.html)
10. Los Angeles Sheriff's Department (2003) *Year in Review: 2002.* Available online at www.lasd.org

11. Los Angeles Sheriff's Department Custody Operations Division web page
12. *Ibid*
13. California Department of Corrections home page (http://www.cdc.state.ca.us/default.asp)
14. *Ibid*
15. Prison Industry Authority home page (http://www.pia.ca.gov/piawebdev/index.html)
16. California Department of Corrections home page
17. California Board of Prison Terms home page (http://www.bpt.ca.gov/index.html)
18. PC §5075
19. California Board of Prison Terms home page
20. California Department of Corrections Parolee Handbook (http://www.cdc.state.ca.us/ParoleDiv/Handbook/Conditions_ex.asp)
21. California Department of Corrections home page
22. Los Angeles County Probation Department home page (http://probation.co.la.ca.us/)
23. San Francisco County Adult Probation Department home page (http://sfprospector.com/site/adultprobation_index.asp?id=80)
24. Superior Court of California, County of San Francisco (2002, June). *San Francisco Adult Probation Department.* Available online at (http://www.sfgov.org/site/courts_page.asp?id=3706)
25. California Department of Corrections home page
26. *Ibid*
27. *Ibid*
28. *Ibid*
29. *Ibid*

CHAPTER 9

THE JUVENILE JUSTICE SYSTEM IN CALIFORNIA

INTRODUCTION

The **juvenile justice system** in California focuses on individuals who have committed crimes and who have not yet reached the age of 18. The system works at all levels of government: city, county, and state. The goal of the system is the treatment and rehabilitation of juvenile offenders. This is different from the adult system, which considers punishment to be the primary goal of sentencing.[1] Because of this difference, many more agencies and organizations participate in the juvenile than the adult justice system, including community organizations, schools, social service agencies, religious organizations, and many others.

The issue of which juveniles fall under the authority of the juvenile justice system for violating the law is discussed in §602(a) of the Welfare and Institutions Code (WIC):

> Except as provided in subdivision (b), any person who is under the age of 18 years when he or she violates any law of this state or of the United States or any ordinance of any city or county of this state defining crime other than an ordinance establishing a curfew based solely on age, is within the jurisdiction of the juvenile court, which may adjudge such person to be a ward of the court.

The juvenile court also has jurisdiction over other categories of juveniles. According to WIC §601(a),

> Any person under the age of 18 years who persistently or habitually refuses to obey the reasonable and proper orders or directions of his or her parents, guardian, or custodian, or who is beyond the control of that person, or who is under the age of 18 years when he or she violated any ordinance of any city or county of this state establishing a curfew based solely on age is within the jurisdiction of the juvenile court which may adjudge the minor to be a ward of the court.

THE JUVENILE JUSTICE PROCESS IN CALIFORNIA

The **arrest** of a juvenile offender is discussed in WIC §625, which states:

> A peace officer may, without a warrant, take into temporary custody a minor:
> (a) Who is under the age of 18 years when such officer has reasonable cause for believing that such minor is a person described in Section 601 or 602, or
> (b) Who is a ward of the juvenile court or concerning whom an order has been made under Section 636 or 702, when such officer has reasonable cause for

believing that person has violated an order of the juvenile court or has escaped from any commitment ordered by the juvenile court, or

(c) Who is under the age of 18 years and who is found in any street or public place suffering from any sickness or injury which requires care, medical treatment, hospitalization, or other remedial care.

In any case where a minor is taken into temporary custody on the ground that there is reasonable cause for believing that such minor is a person described in Section 601 or 602, or that he has violated an order of the juvenile court or escaped from any commitment ordered by the juvenile court, the officer shall advise such minor that anything he says can be used against him and shall advise him of his constitutional rights, including his right to remain silent, his right to have counsel present during any interrogation, and his right to have counsel appointed if he is unable to afford counsel.

The statute specifically requires only reasonable cause, rather than probable cause or the officer's presence during the commission of the offense.

The arresting officer is limited by statute as to what may be done with the juvenile who has been arrested under the provisions of WIC §625. According to WIC §626, the arresting officer has four main options:

1. The officer may release the juvenile.

2. The officer may take or refer the juvenile to an agency, either public or private, that provides shelter, care, counseling, and/or diversion services to such juveniles. The agency must be one with which the city or county has an agreement to provide these services.

3. The officer may prepare a written notice outlining the reasons why the juvenile was taken into custody and requiring the juvenile to appear before a probation officer at a specified time and place. One copy of the notice is to be given to the juvenile's parent or guardian and another to the probation officer. Once the juvenile's parent or guardian has signed a written promise that the juvenile will appear at the appointed time, the juvenile will be released from custody.

4. The officer may turn custody of the juvenile over to a probation officer. If the officer chooses this option, and if the arrest was made without a warrant, delivery of the juvenile must must take place within 24 hours of the arrest. The officer shall also provide a written statement that includes the reasons for taking the juvenile into custody and the probable cause upon which the arrest was based.

According to the statute, when choosing one of these four options, "the officer shall prefer the alternative which least restricts the minor's freedom of movement, provided that alternative is compatible with the best interests of the minor and the community."

In most cases, the officer will refer the juvenile to the probation department. This may be done either through a **non-detained petition request** (option 3 above) or a **detained petition**

request (option 4 above). The juvenile will be transferred to juvenile hall and assigned a probation officer who will be responsible for the juvenile throughout the process. The probation officer is responsible for investigating the alleged violation of the law and for developing a plan that will not only help the child and his or her family but will also best serve the community as a whole.

Many of the responsibilities of the probation officer towards the juvenile are specifically outlined by statute. WIC §627.5 requires that when the juvenile is taken before the probation officer, the officer must immediately advise the juvenile and his or her parent or guardian of the juvenile's constitutional rights. These include

- informing them that anything the juvenile says can be used against him or her
- informing them that the juvenile has the right to remain silent
- informing them that the juvenile has the right to have an attorney present during any questioning
- informing them that the juvenile has the right to have an attorney appointed if they are unable to afford one.

In the case of a non-detained petition request, the juvenile is allowed to return to the home of a parent or guardian. If the officer made a detained petition request, the probation officer will immediately investigate the circumstances and facts surrounding the arrest. Essentially, the officer conducts a risk assessment to determine whether it is necessary to keep the juvenile in custody. The probation officer is required by statute to release the juvenile into the custody of a parent or guardian, unless one or more of the following conditions exist:

> (1) The minor is in need of proper and effective parental care or control and has no parent, legal guardian, or responsible relative; or has no parent, legal guardian, or responsible relative willing to exercise or capable of exercising that care or control; or has no parent, legal guardian, or responsible relative actually exercising that care or control.
> (2) The minor is destitute or is not provided with the necessities of life or is not provided with a home or suitable place of abode.
> (3) The minor is provided with a home which is an unfit place for him or her by reason of neglect, cruelty, depravity or physical abuse by either of his or her parents, or by his or her legal guardian or other person in whose custody or care he or she is entrusted.
> (4) Continued detention of the minor is a matter of immediate and urgent necessity for the protection of the minor or reasonable necessity for the protection of the person or property of another.
> (5) The minor is likely to flee the jurisdiction of the court.
> (6) The minor has violated an order of the juvenile court.
> (7) The minor is physically dangerous to the public because of a mental or physical deficiency, disorder or abnormality.[2]

At least one of these criteria must exist for the probation officer to place a juvenile in a detention facility or "Juvenile Hall". **Juvenile Hall** is essentially the equivalent of an adult **jail**.

If the offender is placed in juvenile hall, the probation department and the district attorney may choose to file a petition with the juvenile court. The district attorney also has the option of requesting that the juvenile be remanded to adult court because, due to the nature of the offense committed, he or she is unfit to be adjudicated as a juvenile.

A **petition** filed with the juvenile court essentially asks the court to get involved in the case. There are two types of petitions. A **"601 Petition"** may be filed by the probation department or by the district attorney's office and alleges that the juvenile committed a status offense, such as running away, skipping school, breaking curfew, or habitually disobeying his or her parents.[3] A **"602 Petition"** is filed by the district attorney's office and alleges that the juvenile engaged in an act that would still be a crime if he or she was an adult (a felony or a misdemeanor).[4] A petition is an accusation, not a conviction. A copy of the petition, and a notice of a juvenile court hearing, will be provided to the juvenile's parent or guardian (and directly to any juvenile who is at least eight years of age).[5]

There are a variety of hearings that may be held in juvenile court. A **Detention Hearing** is held for juveniles who have been held in custody for at least two days. At this time, the judge will decide if the juvenile is to remain in detention or be released to the custody of a parent or guardian before the next hearing. The detention hearing is basically equivalent to an **arraignment** in adult court. A **Pretrial Conference** is not mandatory but is an attempt to settle the problem out of court and avoid formal juvenile court processing. Options that may be considered at a pretrial conference include a reprimand from the probation officer, informal probation, referring the juvenile to a public or private social agency, or placing the juvenile in some voluntary program (e.g., attending substance abuse classes, performing community service, going to a peer court).[6]

California law considers all individuals under the age of 18 to be juveniles. However, in some cases the juvenile court may wish to consider sending a juvenile to be tried at the adult court. This is done through a **fitness hearing**, which is held to determine whether a juvenile will be tried as a juvenile or as an adult.[7] A fitness hearing is only held in cases in which a 602 petition was filed (juveniles accused of status offenses in 601 petitions may not be remanded to adult court). According to WIC §707(a)(1), the court must make the determination of fitness based on the following criteria:

(1) The degree of criminal sophistication exhibited by the minor.
(2) Whether the minor can be rehabilitated prior to the expiration of the juvenile court's jurisdiction.
(3) The minor's previous delinquent history.
(4) Success of previous attempts by the juvenile court to rehabilitate the minor.
(5) The circumstances and gravity of the offense alleged in the petition to have been committed by the minor.

In California, no juvenile under the age of 14 may be remanded to adult court. However, juveniles under the age of 16 may only be considered for trial in an adult court if at least one of the following circumstances are found:

(A) The minor is alleged to have committed an offense which if committed by an adult would be punishable by death or imprisonment in the state prison for life.

(B) The minor is alleged to have personally used a firearm during the commission or attempted commission of a felony...

(C) The minor is alleged to have committed an offense listed in subdivision (b) in which any one or more of the following circumstances apply:

(i) The minor has previously been found to be a person described in Section 602 by reason of the commission of an offense listed in subdivision (b).

(ii) The offense was committed for the benefit of, at the direction of, or in association with any criminal street gang ... with the specific intent to promote, further, or assist in any criminal conduct by gang members.

(iii) The offense was committed for the purpose of intimidating or interfering with any other person's free exercise or enjoyment of any right secured to him or her by the Constitution or laws of this state or by the Constitution or laws of the United States and because of the other person's race, color, religion, ancestry, national origin, disability, gender, or sexual orientation, or because the minor perceives that the other person has one or more of those characteristics ...

(iv) The victim of the offense was 65 years of age or older, or blind, deaf, quadriplegic, paraplegic, developmentally disabled, or confined to a wheelchair, and that disability was known or reasonably should have been known to the minor at the time of the commission of the offense.[8]

Juveniles tried in adult court and found guilty may be sent to an adult prison, rather than being placed in the custody of the California Youth Authority, if they are at least 16 years of age. Juveniles between the ages of 14 and 16 must be sent to the California Youth Authority, even if they are sentenced to an adult prison. However, upon reaching the age of 16, the juvenile may be transferred to an adult facility and placed under the custody of the California Department of Corrections.

A **jurisdiction hearing** is the equivalent of an adult court **trial**. At this stage, the juvenile pleads guilty or not guilty to the petition and the judge hears evidence and testimony. The process is similar to the adult trial procedure, with the district attorney presenting evidence against the juvenile and the juvenile's lawyer presenting evidence in the juvenile's defense. If the judge considers that the evidence is sufficient to find that the juvenile did commit the acts of which he or she was accused in the petition, the judge will make a **true finding**. If there is insufficient evidence to find that the juvenile committed the acts of which he or she was accused, the judge will dismiss the case and, if the juvenile was held in detention, he or she will be released. If the judge makes a true finding, a **disposition hearing** will be held to determine the punishment assigned to the juvenile. This hearing may be held on the same day as the jurisdiction hearing and is the juvenile court equivalent of the adult court **sentencing hearing**. Obviously, if the judge at the jurisdiction hearing finds that the juvenile did not commit the crime, no disposition hearing will be held. Finally, in some counties, **review hearings** are held to monitor the juvenile's progress through disposition.[9]

If the juvenile has been found responsible for the acts of which he or she has been accused, the judge has a variety of options at the disposition hearing. These include:

1. Placing the juvenile on probation in the home of the parent or guardian
2. Placing the juvenile on probation in the home of another relative, in an institution, or in a group home
3. Placing the juvenile on probation in a ranch or probation camp
4. Sending the juvenile to the California Youth Authority
5. Requiring the parent or guardian to attend counseling or parent training.[10]

JUVENILE SUPERVISION IN CALIFORNIA

The California Youth Authority

The history of juvenile supervision by the state can be traced back to 1859, when the San Francisco Industrial School was created by the state Legislature. Prior to this time there were no special juvenile correctional facilities; juvenile boys as young as 12 were placed in San Quentin and Folsom State Prisons. The School housed boys and girls up to the age of 18 and required them to work and attend school. Children were released from the School in one of three ways: discharge, indenture, or leave of absence. Girls were later transferred to the Magdalen Asylum in San Francisco. Over the years a number of other similar "reform schools" were opened. In 1903, California enacted the Juvenile Court Act, establishing juvenile courts in the state. County juvenile halls were established in 1909 to house juveniles awaiting hearings. The first juvenile probation office was created in 1929.[11]

In 1941, the State Legislature passed the **Youth Corrections Authority Act**[12], creating the Youth Corrections Authority. In 1943 the word "Corrections" was dropped, resulting in the current **California Youth Authority** (CYA). According to the CYA website, the Youth Corrections Authority Act:

1. Created a three-person commission appointed by the governor and confirmed by the Senate.
2. Mandated acceptance of all commitments under 23 years of age, including those from Juvenile Court.
3. Added a section on delinquency prevention.
4. Authorized no authority over existing state institutions.
5. Appropriated $100,000 to run the Authority for two years.[13]

The first juvenile ward to be committed under this act was transferred from San Quentin to the CYA's Youth Authority Unit diagnostic facility in 1942. He was a male juvenile who had been convicted of the second degree murder of an uncle and sentenced to life in prison.

In 1943, the CYA was given the responsibility for delinquency prevention as well as taking over the management of three state reformatories providing institutional training and parole supervision for juvenile and young adult offenders. Over the years, the size and role of the CYA has expanded significantly.

Today, the CYA is the largest young offender agency in the country. Its mission, which is stated in WIC §1700, is to "protect society from the consequences of criminal activity." The CYA is responsible for supervising offenders between the ages of 12 and 25 who are housed in juvenile institutions and camps and for juveniles on parole. Juveniles may be sent to CYA facilities from both the juvenile and adult criminal courts. There are three ways in which a juvenile offender may be sent to CYA. First, the juvenile may be committed to a CYA facility by a juvenile court. Second, the juvenile may be tried as an adult and committed to a CYA facility by an adult criminal court. Finally, the juvenile may be tried as an adult and committed to a California Department of Corrections (CDC) facility but ordered housed in a CYA facility for some period of time. Juveniles in this last category are called "M-cases" and may be transferred to an adult CDC facility on or before their 18th birthday.[14]

Offenders who are committed to the CYA are given indeterminate sentences. Parole release is determined by the **Youthful Offender Parole Board**, a separate administrative agency. Determination of the parole release date is based on the severity of the offense committed and the juvenile's progress towards parole readiness.

The CYA operates a total of 11 institutions, 4 camps, and 16 parole offices located throughout the state. The budget for the 2002-2003 fiscal year was $356.4 million. The average cost to house a ward is $49,200 per year.[15] The CYA operates a wide variety of special programs, including treatment for sex offenders, anger management courses, programs on the impact of crime on victims, substance abuse treatment programs, classes for Young Men as Fathers, and programs for seriously emotionally disturbed juveniles. All offenders attend school full time. If they complete high school, they are given the opportunity to participate in vocational and/or college training. Many resident juveniles also work at paid jobs within the institution and a portion of their wages goes to pay court-ordered restitution

In 2002, the CYA supervised an institution population of 5,945 and a parole population of 4,237. CYA populations have been decreasing steadily since the mid-1990s. Among CYA wards who are resident in institutions, the majority (95 percent) are male. Approximately 16 percent are white, 29 percent are black, 48 percent are Hispanic, and 4 percent are Asian. Approximately 59 percent of offenders were institutionalized primarily for violent crimes, 25 percent for property offenses, 4 percent for narcotics and drug offenses, and 12 percent for other offenses. The average age of the institutional population is 19 years of age.[16]

Among CYA wards on parole, approximately 94 percent are male. Approximately 14 percent are white, 25 percent black, 51 percent Hispanic, and 8 percent Asian. Approximately 70 percent were on parole for violent offenses, 21 percent for property offenses, 3 percent for narcotics and drug offenses, and 6 percent for other offenses. The average age of parolees is 21.5 years of age.[17]

The Youthful Offender Parole Board

The **Youthful Offender Parole Board** (YOPB) is responsible for determining the length of confinement for juvenile offenders committed to the CYA. The Board is composed of seven members who are appointed by the governor with the advice and consent of the Senate. Each member serves a term of four years.[18] According to WIC §1719, the Board has the following powers and duties:

> return of persons to the court of commitment for redisposition by the court, discharge of commitment, orders to parole and conditions thereof, revocation or suspension of parole, recommendation for treatment program, determination of the date of next appearance, return of nonresident persons to the jurisdiction of the state of legal residence.

The primary responsibility of the Board is the protection of the public. The Board also emphasizes the creation of offender accountability and the reduction of recidivism. During the 2001-2002 fiscal year, the Board conducted 19,733 parole hearings. If the offender is released on parole, the Board is responsible for setting conditions of parole.[19]

NOTES

1. PC §1170(a)(1)
2. WIC §628(a)
3. WIC §650(a)-(b)
4. WIC §650(c)
5. California Courts Self Help Center: Families and Children web site (http://www.courtinfo.ca.gov/selfhelp/family/)
6. *Ibid*
7. *Ibid*
8. WIC §707(d)(2)
9. California Courts Self Help Center: Families and Children web site
10. *Ibid*
11. California Youth Authority home page (http://www.cya.ca.gov/)
12. WIC Division 2.5, Chapter 1
13. California Youth Authority home page
14. *Ibid*
15. *Ibid*
16. Department of the Youth Authority (2003). *A Comparison of the Youth Authority's Institution and Parole Populations: June 30 Each Year, 1993-2002.* Available online at (http://www.cya.ca.gov/research/pops_93-02.pdf)
17. *Ibid*
18. WIC §1716(a)
19. Youthful Offender Parole Board home page (http://www.yopb.ca.gov/index.html)

CHAPTER 10

DRUGS AND CRIME IN CALIFORNIA

INTRODUCTION

Drug abuse is a serious problem in California. Not only are cocaine, heroin, marijuana, and other drugs brought into the state from Mexico, marijuana is grown in great quantities in California, and methamphetamine is produced in the state as well. During 2000, there were 128,142 felony arrests for drug offenses in California.[1] Of these, 41 percent were for narcotics, 10 percent for marijuana, 45 percent for dangerous drugs, and 3 percent for other drug offenses (this category includes crimes such as manufacturing a controlled substance or forging a narcotics prescription). Approximately 95 percent of the arrests were of adults. Juveniles were most commonly arrested for marijuana. The arrest rate for all categories except that of other drug offenses has decreased significantly since 1995.[2]

There appears to be a definite relationship between drugs and crime. A recent study found that found that in 2000, 65 percent of adult males arrested in San Diego tested positive for drugs at the time of the arrest. In Sacramento, 73 percent of adult males arrested in 2000 tested positive for drugs, and in San Jose, the figure was 52 percent. In all cities, the most commonly used drug was marijuana.[3] According to the California Department of Corrections (DOC), during the year 2000, over 27 percent of all inmates admitted to prison were charged with drug offenses. The most common was possession of a controlled substance.[4] Between 1981 and 2000 there was a general increase in drug offenses. However, between 2000 and 2001, there was a clear decrease in drug offenses, particularly among female offenders. In 2000, 42 percent of female offenders were incarcerated for drug offenses; in 2001, this figure had declined to 35.1 percent. The decline in drug offenses among male offenders was much less marked: the figure dropped from 26 percent in 2000 to almost 24 percent in 2001.[5] Of course, these figures do not include offenders who, while not arrested for or convicted of drug offenses, are still committing crimes that are related to drug abuse, such as crimes committed to obtain money to obtain drugs.

THE AVAILABILITY OF DRUGS IN CALIFORNIA

Marijuana

According to the U.S. Drug Enforcement Administration (DEA), **marijuana** is the most commonly abused illegal drug in California. Marijuana is grown in California as well as being transported into the state across the Mexican border. Much of the domestic marijuana is grown in indoor hydroponic gardens, and cultivation has increased significantly since the 1996 passage of Proposition 215, the Compassionate Use Act, which legalized the use of marijuana for certain specific medical conditions.[6] Domestic marijuana tends to be preferred by users because of its higher levels of THC and costs between $4,000 and $6,000 per pound.[7]

Cocaine

Cocaine is readily available in California. It is frequently smuggled into the state from Mexico and shipped around the United States.[8] The price and purity level vary around the state. In northern California, the price of a kilogram of cocaine ranges from $14,000 to $22,000 while in central California, prices range from $13,700 to $17,000. Both powder and crack cocaine are available, as well as "speedballs", which is a combination of heroin and cocaine.[9]

Heroin

Heroin is smuggled into California from Mexico, Colombia, and Southeast Asia, with Mexican black tar heroin being the most commonly-available and inexpensive type. Purity levels are increasing, so users can snort the drug rather than being forced to inject it.[10] In southern California, one kilogram of pure (79 percent) black tar heroin may sell from between $40,000 and $75,000 dollars, with an ounce costing between $800 and $1,450.[11]

Methamphetamine

The DEA considers **methamphetamine** to be the primary drug threat in California. The drug is produced in Mexico and smuggled across the border.[12] In addition, northern California, particularly the San Francisco Bay area has become an important area for the production of high-quality methamphetamine. San Diego is also a major center for methamphetamine production. Crystal methamphetamine, or "ice" is readily available in central California, with purity levels of 85 to 100 percent. Methamphetamine sells for between $80 and $100 per gram.[13]

Club Drugs

Club drugs include a number of illegal drugs that are found at nightclubs and "raves". The three most common club drugs are MDMA (Ecstacy), Ketamine, and GHB. Other club drugs available in California include LSD, Rohypnol, and OxyContin. Ecstacy appears to be the most popular and widely available club drug in California and is most commonly used by adolescents. It is often taken together with marijuana, alcohol, GBH, or methamphetamine.[14]

CALIFORNIA DRUG TREATMENT COURTS

Drug courts were first developed in Florida in the early 1990s as a way of diverting drug offenders out of traditional criminal justice prosecution. They handle cases involving drug-addicted offenders through the use of extensive supervision and treatment. They also attempt to increase the coordination of various agencies and resources available to drug abusers, increase the cost-effectiveness of the programs, and provide the offender with access to a wide variety of programs and resources. The first adult drug court in California was developed in 1991 in Alameda County. The first drug court for juveniles was begun in 1995 in Tulare County. As of July 2002, there were a total of 135 adult and juvenile drug courts in 50 counties in California.[15]

According to the California Department of Alcohol and Drug Programs, the goals of drug court programs in California are to:

- reduce drug usage and recidivism;
- provide court supervised treatment;

- offer the capability to integrate drug treatment with other rehabilitation services to promote long-term recovery and reduce social costs; and
- access federal and State support for local drug courts.[16]

There are four main types or models of drug courts found in California. The first type is a **pre-plea model**, which diverts defendants charged with drug possession before they are prosecuted. If the defendant participates in and successfully completes a drug treatment program supervised by the drug court, he/she will be released without a criminal record. Those who fail to successfully complete the program will be charged and tried. In a **post-plea model**, the defendant is required to plead guilty to the drug charge or charges before being placed in the drug court program. Again, if the defendant successfully completes the program, all criminal charges will be dismissed. However, if the defendant fails to complete the program, he/she is sentenced for the charge or charges to which he/she has already pled guilty. A **post-adjudication model** focuses on repeat drug offenders who have already been convicted of drug offenses but who have not yet served their sentences. If the offender successfully completes the program, he/she is allowed to serve the sentence in treatment rather than in custody. An offender who fails to complete the program is returned to the jail or prison to serve his/her sentence. Finally, the **civil model** was developed for individuals involved in various civil actions, such as child custody battles. The individual is allowed to enter drug treatment as a condition of getting or keeping child custody. If the individual fails to complete the program, he/she will permanently lose custody of the child.

The pre-plea model is specifically discussed in PC §1000.5. According to the statute,

> criminal proceedings are suspended without a plea of guilty for designated defendants. The drug court program shall include a regimen of graduated sanctions and rewards, individual and group therapy, urine analysis testing commensurate with treatment needs, close court monitoring and supervision of progress, educational or vocational counseling as appropriate, and other requirements as agreed to by the presiding judge or his or her designee, the district attorney, and the public defender.[17]

The suspension of criminal proceedings is contingent upon the defendant's performance in the program. If the defendant performs satisfactorily throughout the court-assigned treatment and completes the program successfully, all charges will be dismissed. However, if the court finds that the defendant is not performing satisfactorily in the assigned treatment program, is not benefitting from the education, treatment, or rehabilitation provided by the program, or has committed another crime which makes him or her unsuitable for the pre-guilty plea program, the court may restore the original criminal charges.[18]

Drug courts in California serve a wide variety of populations. Some focus on juveniles, others on adults. Others specifically target probation violators, repeat drug offenders, or multiple offenders. Most participants have not received substance abuse treatment prior to their participation in the drug court program.[19] Drug courts are highly cost-effective, especially compared with traditional offender incarceration. The cost of treating a defendant in a drug court program ranges from $900 to $1,600. The cost of incarcerating that same defendant averages $5,000.[20]

THE SUBSTANCE ABUSE AND CRIME PREVENTION ACT OF 2000

In November, 2000, California passed Proposition 36, the Substance Abuse and Crime Prevention Act (SACPA). The law, which emphasizes rehabilitation, has significantly changed how many drug offenders are treated in the state. The Act diverts certain non-violent adult offenders who have been convicted of drug use or possession out of the prison and jail system and into community-based drug treatment programs. This not only helps to reduce the problem of prison and jail overcrowding and reserve scarce incarceration resources for serious violent offenders, but also focuses on reducing the problems of drug abuse and drug-related crime by allowing offenders to participate in more effective treatment programs than they might otherwise receive.

Offenders who are eligible for treatment under the Act will be sentenced to probation and will receive up to one year of community-based drug treatment and an additional six months of after-care. Participants in the program may also receive other services, such as vocational training, education, and family counseling. The drug treatment will be considered a condition of probation.

Offenders who are eligible for the program include those convicted of a first or second non-violent drug use or possession offense. In addition, individuals who are on probation or parole for certain non-violent offenses and who violate a drug-related condition of their probation or parole may be eligible to receive community-based treatment instead of being sent to jail or prison. The following offenders are excluded from the program:

- any offender who has been convicted of a serious or violent felony during the last five years
- any offender who was convicted of a felony or a non-drug related misdemeanor in the same court proceeding as the drug offense
- any offender who used a firearm while under the influence or who possessed cocaine, heroin, methamphetamine, or phencyclidine
- any offender who refused drug treatment as a condition of probation[21]

There are several key differences between SACPA and the drug treatment courts that already exist in California. First of all, while drug courts are county-based, and are not present in all 58 counties, SACPA is a state law and thus must be implemented throughout the entire state. Similarly, the provisions of the Act are uniform throughout California, while every drug court is a separate entity, with its own eligibility requirements and program options. In addition, unlike drug courts, which only admit a small number of eligible offenders, SACPA programs are required to provide treatment to all offenders who commit an eligible offense. Another difference is that drug court programs include pre-conviction diversion while SACPA programs only include individuals who have been convicted by the courts.[22]

NOTES

1. Office of National Drug Control Policy, Drug Policy Information Clearinghouse (2002, May). *State of California: Profile of Drug Indicators.*

(http://www.whitehousedrugpolicy.gov/statelocal/ca/ca.pdf)
2. California Department of Justice (2001). *Crime and Delinquency in California, 2000.*
3. Office of National Drug Control Policy, Drug Policy Information Clearinghouse (2002, May). *State of California: Profile of Drug Indicators.*
4. State of California, Department of Corrections (2001). *California Prisoners and Parolees, 2001.* (http://www.cdc.state.ca.us)
5. California Department of Corrections (2002). *Historical Trends: 1981-2001.* (http://www.cdc.state.ca.us)
6. DEA Fact Sheet: *California.* (http://www.usdoj.gov/dea/pubs/states/california.html)
7. Office of National Drug Control Policy, Drug Policy Information Clearinghouse (2002, May). *State of California: Profile of Drug Indicators.*
8. DEA Fact Sheet: *California.*
9. Office of National Drug Control Policy, Drug Policy Information Clearinghouse (2002, May). *State of California: Profile of Drug Indicators.*
10. DEA Fact Sheet: *California.*
11. Office of National Drug Control Policy, Drug Policy Information Clearinghouse (2002, May). *State of California: Profile of Drug Indicators.*
12. DEA Fact Sheet: *California.*
13. Office of National Drug Control Policy, Drug Policy Information Clearinghouse (2002, May). *State of California: Profile of Drug Indicators.*
14. DEA Fact Sheet: *California.*
15. California Department of Alcohol and Drug Programs (2002, July). *Fact Sheet: Drug Court Programs.* (http://www.adp.cahwnet.gov/FactSheets/Drug_Court_Programs.pdf)
16. *Ibid*
17. PC §1000.5(a)
18. PC §1000.5(b)
19. California Department of Alcohol and Drug Programs (2002, July). *Fact Sheet: Drug Court Programs.*
20. California Courts: *Drug Courts* (http://www.courtinfo.ca.gov/programs/drugcourts/about.htm)
21. California Courts: *Highlights of Proposition 36: The Substance Abuse and Crime Prevention Act (*http://www.courtinfo.ca.gov/programs/drugcourts/documents/highlights.pdf)
22. Uelman, Gerald (2002, March). *Substance Abuse and Crime Prevention Act of 2000: Progress Report.* Sacramento: Drug Policy Alliance. (http://www.prop36.org/pdf/Prop36Report.pdf)

APPENDIX

WEBSITES OF INTEREST

There is a wealth of information on California and the California criminal justice system available on the worldwide web. Below is a selection of web sites that may be of interest to students.

GENERAL CALIFORNIA WEB SITES

http://www.ca.gov/state/portal/myca_homepage.jsp
The official home page of the State of California. It provides a variety of information services for citizens regarding California history, government, and much more.

http://caag.state.ca.us/cjsc/index.htm
The Criminal Justice Statistics Center is run by the California Department of Justice and contains data on subjects such as arrests, convictions, and commitments in California.

http://www.ocjp.ca.gov/
The Governor's Office of Criminal Justice Planning develops and implements criminal justice policy state-wide.

LEGAL INFORMATION

http://www.leginfo.ca.gov/calaw.html
This website provides access to all 29 California legal codes and to the California State Constitution.

http://ccr.oal.ca.gov/
The California Code of Regulations consists of all regulations that have been formally adopted by the state. It includes, among other things, the regulations governing the California Board of Prison Terms.

http://www.courtinfo.ca.gov/rules/
This website provides access to the California Rules of Court

INFORMATION ON POLICE IN FLORIDA

http://www.clew.org/
This private website contains links to over 350 California police departments and law enforcement agencies

http://www.chp.ca.gov/

The home page of the California Highway Patrol.

http://www.lapdonline.org/index.htm

The home page of the Los Angeles Police Department.

http://www.lasd.org/

The home page of the Los Angeles County Sheriff's Department

http://www.ci.sf.ca.us/sheriff/home.htm

The home page of the San Francisco Sheriff's Department

http://www.post.ca.gov/

The home page of the California Commission on Police Officer Standards and Training

INFORMATION ON THE CALIFORNIA COURT SYSTEM

http://www.courtinfo.ca.gov/

The home page of the California court system

http://caag.state.ca.us/

The home page of the California Office of the Attorney General

http://www.calbar.ca.gov/state/calbar/calbar_home.jsp

The home page of the State Bar of California

http://www.ospd.ca.gov/

The home page of the Office of the State Public Defender

http://www.boc.cahwnet.gov/

The home page of the Victim Compensation and Government Claims Board

INFORMATION ON CORRECTIONS IN CALIFORNIA

http://www.cdc.state.ca.us/

The home page of the California Department of Corrections.

http://www.bdcorr.ca.gov/

The home page of the California Board of Corrections.

http://www.yaca.state.ca.us/

The home page of the California Youth and Adult Correctional Agency

http://www.bpt.ca.gov/
The home page of the California Board of Prison Terms

http://www.pia.ca.gov/piawebdev/index.html
The home page of the Prison Industry Authority

http://www.cdc.state.ca.us/ParoleDiv/Handbook/handbook.asp
The California Department of Corrections *Parolee Handbook* is available online

http://probation.co.la.ca.us/
The home page of the Los Angeles County Probation Department

http://www.cdc.state.ca.us/communicationsoffice/capitalpunishment/default.asp
The California Department of Corrections home page has a considerable amount of information on capital punishment in California

INFORMATION ON JUVENILE JUSTICE IN CALIFORNIA

http://www.cya.ca.gov/
The home page for the California Youth Authority

http://www.courtinfo.ca.gov/selfhelp/family/delinq/index.htm
The California Courts website has a considerable amount of information on the juvenile court system in California

http://www.yopb.ca.gov/
The home page of the Youthful Offenders Parole Board

INFORMATION ON DRUGS IN CALIFORNIA

http://www.adp.cahwnet.gov/
The home page of the California Department of Alcohol and Drug Programs

http://www.dss.cahwnet.gov/cdssweb/
The home page of the California Department of Social Services

http://www.usdoj.gov/dea/pubs/states/california.html
A federal Drug Enforcement Agency factsheet on drugs in California

http://www.courtinfo.ca.gov/programs/drugcourts/
The California Courts website has a section devoted to drug courts in California